What 16,944 individuals can tell us about why they do, *or don't,* affiliate.

THE DECISION TO JOIN

How individuals determine value and why they choose to belong

JAMES DALTON AND MONICA DIGNAM

RESEARCH AND ANALYSIS FROM ASAE & THE CENTER FOR ASSOCIATION LEADERSHIP

asae & the center™
for association leadership

WASHINGTON, D.C.

Information in this book is accurate as of the time of publication and consistent with standards of good practice in the general management community. As research and practice advance, however, standards may change. For this reason, it is recommended that readers evaluate the applicability of any recommendation in light of particular situations and changing standards.

ASAE & The Center for Association Leadership
1575 I Street, NW
Washington, DC 20005-1103
Phone: 202-371-0940 (when calling from within the Washington, D.C., metropolitan area)
Phone: 888-950-2723 (when calling from outside the Washington, D.C., metropolitan area)
Fax: 202-408-9634
Email: books@asaecenter.org

ASAE & The Center For Association Leadership connect great ideas to great people to inspire leadership and achievement within the association community.

John H. Graham IV, CAE, President and CEO, ASAE
Susan Sarfati, CAE, President and CEO, The Center for Association Leadership and Executive Vice President, ASAE
Susan Robertson, Senior Vice President, ASAE & The Center for Association Leadership
Monica Dignam, Vice President, Industry & Market Research, ASAE & The Center for Association Leadership
Clare Inzeo, Research Associate, Industry & Market Research, ASAE & The Center for Association Leadership
Keith C. Skillman, CAE, Vice President, Publications, ASAE & The Center for Association Leadership
Baron Williams, Director, Book Publishing, ASAE & The Center for Association Leadership

A complete catalog of ASAE titles is available on the Web at **www.asaecenter.org/bookstore**.

Cover design by Beth Lower
Interior design by Cimarron Design

International Standard Book Number-10 digit: 0-88034-286-2
International Standard Book Number-13 digit: 978-0-88034-286-5

Printed in the United States of America.

Table of Contents

Table of Exhibits

Acknowledgements

I N THE TRUEST SPIRIT of association, *The Decision to Join* has been a collaborative effort, involving many and for "the good of the order." ASAE & The Center for Association Leadership Industry Research prepared the study, working extensively with numerous volunteers and staff. We are ever-grateful to all those who contributed their expertise in support of this study. ASAE & The Center for Association Leadership extend a special thanks to the following organizations and individuals:

Co-sponsors

- American Chemical Society
- American College of Healthcare Executives
- American Geophysical Union
- American Health Information Management Association
- American Society for Quality
- American Society of Civil Engineers
- American Society of Mechanical Engineers
- College of American Pathologists
- Credit Union Executives Society
- Emergency Nurses Association
- IEEE
- Institute of Food Technologists
- National Association of Secondary School Principals
- National Athletic Trainers Association
- National Court Reporters Association
- National Society of Accountants
- Project Management Institute
- School Nutrition Association

Volunteers

We thank the ASAE & The Center for Association Leadership Membership Section Council, and particularly 2006-2007 Chair Sheri Jacobs and council members Jodi Goldberg, Stuart Meyer, and Shelley Sanner. We are equally indebted to Sharon Moss and staff member Carylann Pishner for their work in preparing Appendix C.

We would also like to extend thanks to Sarah Varner, CAE, whose idea it was to take a fresh look at *The Decision to Join*.

And, as always, we express our most sincere appreciation to the association executives and staff who supported this study.

We welcome any comments about the study. Please address comments to ASAE's Industry & Market Research Department at evaluations@asaecenter.org.

What Frames the Individual's Decision to Join

A PERSON'S DECISION TO JOIN an individual membership organization is *not* a cost-benefit analysis.

If not revolutionary, that idea is certainly not the conventional wisdom.[1] After all, we live, work, and recruit among the increasingly self-oriented, right? The membership appeal should be what's in it for them, or so many think. Turns out it isn't that simple. The conclusion that a current or prospective member's choice of whether to affiliate with your association or any other is not a classic procurement consideration is a foundational concept. The reality of this Decision to Join research finding opens the door to insight, refined strategic imperative, and perhaps a revised appeal grounded in what matters most to each segment of a membership organization's constituency.

Historically, associations have offered a unique value proposition that certainly includes the type of benefits considered when comparing the price paid with the individual benefits received. But the decision to join an association reflects an expanded understanding of what constitutes a benefit. It goes beyond the self-oriented assessment of the value received

---

[1] Tschirhart, Mary, "Nonprofit Membership Associations," *The Non-Profit Sector: A Research Handbook,* 2nd edition, Walter W. Powell and Richard Steinberg, editors, Yale University Press, 2006, pp. 523-541. Cost-benefit assumptions were made by one of the earliest empirical researchers to investigate the decision to join an association and subsequently rejected by nearly all who followed. Nonetheless, "the contention remains that joining an association is a calculated self-interested decision."

by the individual making the decision to incorporate a more other-oriented assessment of value generated for a community of interests. In effect, it expands the spectrum of benefits delivered by reversing the polarity on the concept of recipient value. Individuals receive value, and for no additional cost their decision generates value for those who share a common bond. Everyone who contemplates the decision to join may not understand this initially, but nearly all come to see it this way across time. Unfortunately, not everyone who offers the opportunity to join understands it either, which raises a major concern. Clarifying this value spectrum and validating its importance to the intrinsic appeal of associating with others for a common purpose is one of the many challenges this study addresses.

Some Background

Eighteen individual membership organizations pooled their resources to create a diverse population of people who are, were, or could be but never chose to become members of an association. The intent was to replicate a similar survey conducted by ASAE in the 1980s, which led to the original publication of *The Decision to Join*: *Insights Based on a Survey of Association Members and Nonmembers,* published by The Foundation of the American Society of Association Executives in 1981 and reissued in 1986. But fundamental differences between that research study and this current one limit the opportunity to compare findings. The original study had less than 1,000 responses, which was enough for significance as a whole but not large enough to study different decision-making patterns in smaller segmentation cells, such as entry-level professionals versus senior-level managers. With more than 16,000 responses, this survey opened the door to a vast amount of segmenting.

A subtle difference separates these two studies in a far more significant way. The original survey did not examine affiliations with respondents' associations other than the one that provided their names. The effect that this omission had on the suitability of the 1981 data is responsible for a misnomer in the use of the term *nonmember*. Think of it this way: When respondents from a sponsoring association's nonmember population identify themselves as a current member of some other association, they are not really an association "nonmember" because they have, in fact, demonstrated their belief in the value of association membership through their decision to join one. That they are a member of Society A rather than Society B is a footnote in the larger scheme of understanding the decision to join. Those classified as nonmembers in the original study include this type of respondent, which means that study was about the decision to join one association in particular. That narrow focus is of limited value to those who don't care about the foibles of a particular association but are looking for insights on factors that differentiate people who do and do not make affirmative decisions to join. By examining that simple question, this study was able to aggregate the respondents into a normative database that includes current members of any association, former members of some association who are not currently members of any, and a rare but important population of those who have never joined any association. With this information, a study of the decision to join can account for the respondents' full range of association experience, where the infrastructure of 18 sponsoring associations can be made to disappear, leaving an unencumbered view of the essential decision. Or, that very same infrastructure can be invoked to look more closely at the decision to join a particular association. Both the enormity of the respondent database and the versatility that it offers vastly improves the usefulness of this information, but comparison opportunities with the original (1981) study are limited.

A summary of the research method engaged and the sponsoring societies involved is provided in Appendix A. Despite the considerable demographic diversity that the sponsoring associations provided, many association leaders will see differences between their members and the respondent population, which may lead them to believe it has limited relevance to their associations. The first part of that statement is true but the second is false. Every association is different from the respondent population, but the opportunity for insight resides in understanding how any particular association is different and, more importantly, the implications that stem from those distinctions. This is the nature of normative data. Insights flow from understanding the differences.

Strategic Implications of Key Findings

Consider this: If you and everyone in your organization comprehended, at a deep level, the influence of demographic, attitudinal, and other factors on an individual's choice to affiliate—or not—you could

- Improve your association's value proposition.
- Create and execute a more effective strategy.
- Target member and prospect segments, and tailor your offerings, in ways that *most* appeal to them.

The Decision to Join is insight-inciting intelligence to help you on your journey to achieving exactly those things. Chapter 2 provides a review of the primary questions asked and the reasoning that went into their development. The complexity of the survey, both in terms of its range of questioning and the opportunity to cross-tabulate by a wide array of demographic and social characteristics makes this a useful orientation to the remaining chapters. Chapter 3 gives the big view by summarizing how all respondents answered all the questions. This gives a point of comparison to the additional information that was generated in the segmenting and cross-tabulations that are addressed in the remaining chapters. A summary of key findings with chapter references follows:

The Image of Associations

When asked a series of questions about the value of associations in general, the industry gets very strong positive ratings and negatives that are close to negligible. Predictably, current members report the highest positives. Former members have a lower estimation of associations in general than "never" members. Chapter 4 provides details on the types of benefits that have greater appeal to the "never" and former members, which indicate the appeals that might be most appropriate for them.

Reasons for Dropping

Respondents who reported having dropped their membership in an association at any point in their career were asked to give the reasons why. Approximately half of them indicate their reasons had more to do with career and other life changes than with the performance of the association. This means that those who worry about their retention rates get a 50 percent discount on their current distress levels. Reasons that account for the other half of the cup that is indeed empty are enumerated.

Levels of Involvement

The impact that voluntary service has on the perception of value was looked into by segmenting three groups based on levels of involvement and a fourth for those who were not involved. Predictably, respondent perception of value received from their association increases with their level of involvement, but Chapter 4 makes several related observations that are of strategic importance. For example:

- Perception of value rises with involvement to a point where those who govern the association are no longer in sync with the perceptions of the majority who are not involved. This can be a perilous flip in perceptions. In some cases, elected leaders may be aware of this and rightfully attribute the discrepancy to (a) the vantage point they have by virtue of the facts at their disposal and (b) their leadership responsibility to leverage this information in tough decisions that the members may not fully appreciate. Nevertheless, the notion that elected leaders are the unwavering voice of the members may warrant a closer look. It may be useful for leaders to know where they are out of sync with the members and by how much. If nothing else, a well-crafted communication plan based on accurate information can reduce the risks associated with being out of sync.

- Leaders who lament the fact that young people entering the field are difficult to recruit into the association may find it interesting to note that several of the benefits to which they as leaders give low importance ratings are the very ones that those difficult-to-recruit young people rate as the most important. Furthermore, these young people give associations more negative performance ratings on these benefits while the leaders indicate performance is on par with the level of importance. This includes such things as access to career information and employment opportunities. For leaders to know when they are out of sync with strategically important minority groups may be as useful as knowing when they are out of sync with the majority.

- A segment created to differentiate levels of involvement included those who are engaged in ad hoc volunteer activities. As we use the term, *ad hoc volunteers* are those who perform tasks like writing, presenting, or reviewing content, as distinct from volunteers who serve in more formal, ongoing capacities on committees or in governance. Representing 16 percent of the total respondents, the ad hoc group was slightly larger than the combined segments for governance and committee members. These volunteers differ from the other two groups in interesting ways. They place higher importance on networking and lower importance on the legislative and regulatory activities. They appear to provide an important segue between the uninvolved and the committee workforce that many association managers think of as their "volunteers." This raises a question as to the extent to which these ad hoc volunteers are even recognized as a distinct segment or cultivated to become more involved. Doing this effectively might require knowing why they give different value ratings from the other two groups, particularly with respect to the benefits that affect the common good. Cultivating them may require accommodating their priorities or enlightening them on the importance of the common good; or both.

- Whatever is done about ad hoc volunteers, it's certainly worth noting that there is a chasm of difference in the perception of value that is perceived by the majority who are not involved versus the upward slope of enthusiasm that takes off with ad hoc involvement. Those who are not involved lie perilously close to former members in their overarching assessments of the value they derive from associations. If former members are thought of as being dead, the uninvolved are close to comatose. And from that delightful imagery, involvement might be thought of as the life blood of an association, which therefore deserves much more strategic attention than it gets.

Generations

All of the attention that has been given to the unique attributes of younger generations and the adverse effects this may have on the future of associations are not corroborated by these findings. On the contrary, these findings agree with other recent research regarding young peoples' dispositions toward associations and the implications those have on the decision to join. Chapter 5 details these findings and concludes that the traditional model based on the needs that align with the stages in career development is more useful than generational stereotypes. A considerable body of evidence indicates that entry-level people have always been slow to appreciate the value that associations offer until their career pursuits settle in as they reach their late 20s. These findings support that notion with one caveat. They are not satisfied with the effectiveness of associations in meeting the most important needs associated with this career stage, such as opportunities to gain leadership experience. Associations will need to strengthen the services they offer this segment if they intend to offset alternative means of networking and accessing information sources.

Gender

When males and females are compared without regard to their work settings, the differences in the way they discern value from their associations are modest. Women put greater emphasis on the need to take collective actions that will change their environments, while men emphasize the need to acquire information on the environment they are in and the implications that has for them as individuals. But as Chapter 6 explains, when segments are created to look at the impact of gender-dominant environments (defined in this study as associations that serve fields in which three quarters or more of the members are a single gender), quite an array of differences emerge for women in female-dominant settings, as well as women in male-dominant settings and males in male-dominant settings. For example, women in female-dominant settings have a significantly greater sense of value from their associations than women in more integrated settings. Men, on the other hand, report greater association value when working in integrated as opposed to male-dominant settings.

Employment Settings

Chapter 7 looks at a fairly modest set of differences that correlate with employer types, which includes segments for those in the private sector, nonprofits, government, and academia. Two strong messages emerge from this:

- Anecdotal evidence suggests that in some associations, such as those representing research-intensive medical specialties, academic members are held in the highest esteem. In scientific disciplines where most of the research occurs in universities, the academic members are the majority and therefore the norm. But in many other associations, academics are more apt to be seen as a minority marginalized by professorial stereotypes. In these survey findings the academic respondents are the least apt to drop membership, the most apt to volunteer, and far more apt to be promoters of their associations. Given the additional fact that they are in positions to influence those entry-level people who are slow to join associations, some of those stereotypes may be blocking the path to better asset use. Academics are among the strongest association supporters.

- Regardless of employment setting, when employers endorse the value of association memberships through support for dues payments, those members are, not surprisingly, far more likely to retain their memberships. Surprisingly, at least for those who hold to the adage that people who pay for something themselves are more apt to appreciate the value they receive, that thinking does not stand up with respect to payment of membership dues. Respondents whose employers paid for their dues are equally satisfied with the value they receive. But as many association managers are all too keenly aware, the number of employers who are willing to pay association dues is dropping precipitously. Given the increasing level of investment many employers are making in continuing education of their workforce and their apparent need to demonstrate social responsibility—two areas in which associations have strength—one might assume that there is a disconnect in managements' understanding of associations' value proposition. On the other hand, it might be equally true that associations have failed to appreciate employer needs accurately enough to adjust their value propositions sufficiently to make the employer sale on behalf of their employees. Some associations are pursuing such strategies in earnest. But the level of research this may require and the experimenting necessary to hone the appeal may warrant an industrywide collaboration from the association community.

Outside the United States

Chapter 8 raises some interesting concerns for United States associations that are considering more assertive global strategies, particularly for those who have yet to make the reasoning behind these intentions clear to their current United States members. Nearly 20 percent of the respondents to this survey were located outside the United States, but even the enormity of this respondent database meets its match in the size and diversity of the global market for memberships in United States associations. So no claims are made regarding the extent to which these respondents reflect the global market, but they do demonstrate the level of impact members outside the United States can have on the value rating that "the members" give to association benefits. For example:

- Global respondents are far less interested than their domestic counterparts in professional development, possibly due to the distances involved; but they are far more interested in networking, where distance is not incidental. What are they looking for in networking? That question was not addressed in this survey, but it may be something that domestic members would like to know more about.

- Global members have strong interests in ad hoc volunteering, probably as an extension of their networking interests. How easy has the association made it for them to do this? If some combination of electronic media and ad hoc volunteer activities offers a solution to this, are the details worked out as a tactical part of the strategy?

- In the overall importance of benefits that associations offer, domestic members rank the establishment and enforcement of a code of ethics near the very top. When global respondents enter into the equation, the rank order of ethics drops significantly. Have the ramifications of a hit like that been calculated into the democratic imperatives of strategic planning? Will domestic members like the results when they are? Will the people who make those decisions still be in office when they do become aware? Is that an ethical imperative? How do you calculate the proximity of Bastille Day?

Back to the Future of the Good of the Order

The single most important finding of this study may lie in a simple set of metrics that document a point made in the opening of this chapter and expounded upon in Chapter 4. Research done by others who have explored the reasons why people join associations have used terms such as "selective" versus "collective" benefits, or "material" versus "solidarity" gains to get at this same point. Throughout this text, the observations about associations made by Alexis de Tocqueville in *Democracy in America,* 1835, and an American idiom are used to describe the latter concept as the "common good" or the "good of the order." By whatever terms one prefers, any meaningful understanding of an association involves a balancing act between a calculation of what's in it for me and for us. From their contemporary street smarts, many in this industry will argue that those times have changed. People have become much more self-absorbed. Pure cost-benefit is the way to go. This may well be the case, but in the spirit of good research and useful argument one might ask to see the data backing these claims.

In this study, the survey respondents were given two listings of association benefits. One was labeled "personal benefits" and the other "benefits to the field." They were asked to rate the importance of each benefit on a scale of 1–5. The findings from these two questions are summarized for each of the social and demographic segments considered in Chapters 3 through 8. But in the end and overriding all of that segmenting, a mean score was calculated for all respondents on all personal benefits and a similar one was derived for the benefits to the field. The bottom line from the standpoint of these findings is the straightforward fact that all of the personal benefits described received an overall 3.4 importance rating and benefits to the field received a loftier and statistically significant 3.6. That means that the benefits for the good of the order are more important than personal benefits, though both hang closely together, as a good balancing act should. When former members are sorted out to compare with current members, the gap between the two scores narrows a bit for former members, but the good of the order is still greater. Those who have never been members of any association balance the pair in near parity, but the nod still goes to the common good. To the extent that this "never" member segment is slightly biased by a prevalence of younger people, the findings on stages of career development that are provided in Chapter 5 indicate two lessons. Younger people are likely to acquire a stronger appreciation for the common good as they mature. Education on the value of the common good may be necessary to increase the percentage of younger members who retain association memberships once they join. Based on these data, the claim is made that the unity of personal benefits and benefits to the field are the Yin and the Yang of association management. They are the complementary opposites on a spectrum of value.

CHAPTER **2**

The Study Framework

The survey had three primary parts. The first part was referred to as the respondents' predisposition to join, because it asked a series of questions about respondent attitudes toward associations in general. The second part identified the sponsoring association that submitted each respondent's name and asked respondents about their perceptions of the value that a particular association delivers and how those values influence (or would influence in the case of nonmembers) their decision to join. The third part included the demographic questions that were used to generate the cross-tabulations addressed in subsequent chapters. The importance of understanding how the term nonmember *is used in this study is explained in this chapter.*

THE 16,944 PEOPLE WHO responded to this survey will be viewed in this study from many different angles, but first and foremost they should be seen as a very large group of practitioners who are eligible for membership in a voluntary organization that focuses on their field of endeavor. Whether they are current members, former members, members of a competing association, or never a member of anything is—on this first level of analysis—a secondary matter. When seen as one homogeneous group of people who are or could be members, they constitute an opportunity to examine the way membership organizations are seen in general. This panoramic view is aimed at understanding what is referred to as someone's predisposition to join. This is important because the way people characterize associations in general influences the way they are very apt to discern value when facing the decision to join one association in particular.

Predisposition is not a predictor that determines how one will make a decision, because thoughtful people are not always consistent in the way they think. Many automobile consumers tell public policy makers that for the good of the nation, car manufacturers should offer more fuel-efficient vehicles; yet many of these same people fail to demonstrate consistency when buying their own car. Disconnects emerge as decision makers move from predisposition to their actual choices. The car-buying decision illustrates a common disconnect that is a function of the difference between what one truly believes is good for everyone versus what one deems to be good for someone special.

Predisposition is nevertheless important for several reasons. First, inconsistency may be inevitable, but it is not the rule. Predisposition influences rational people in ways that are predictable much of the time, and that alone makes it important in understanding the decision to join an association. Second, understanding an inconsistency adds insight to knowing what is important, because inconsistent thinking is not irrational so much as it is a reflection of the fact that the observer is missing information regarding the decision-making criteria. Finally, the previously mentioned disconnect between knowing what might be good for me and/or them is a traffic circle in which many who navigate the decision to join an association can get hopelessly lost. Understanding predisposition offers the coordinates needed to monitor that traffic pattern.

The framework of this study had three primary parts that were incorporated into the design of the survey and might be thought of as lines of inquiry. (See Appendix B for Frequency Tables for All Questions/All Respondents.)

Part One

The first addressed the value of associations in general and focused on predisposition to join. In this part, the respondents' status as members or nonmembers of the sponsoring society that provided their names was set aside. The demographic information collected in Part Three of the survey was used to reconfigure a respondent's membership status into one of three segments:

- Current member of any association (sponsor or any other)
- Former member of an association, but not currently a member of any
- Never a member of any association

Chapter 4, "Affiliation and Involvement," looks at the way in which these three segments compare in their responses.

Part Two

The second part of the study was based on questions that focused the respondents' attention on the merits of joining or not joining the particular sponsoring association that provided their names, which brings back into

play the more familiar segment configuration of members and nonmembers of a particular association. These two populations received slightly different questionnaires to accommodate questions that were affected by their status—for instance, questions on satisfaction with the association's performance, which nonmembers were not in a position to answer.

Part Three

The third part of the study collected information on respondent demographics and other characteristics used to assemble the segmentation schemes that were used to create the mosaic of observations on factors that influence the decision to join.

The remainder of this chapter elaborates on these three parts by deconstructing the survey questions to explain the thinking behind them and provide context that should expedite the reader's grasp of segment-oriented observations provided in the remaining chapters.

The Value of Associations in General

The survey questions that were designed to probe the respondents' attitudes toward associations in general did so by looking into three areas: overarching value, predisposition, and environmental challenges.

Overarching Value

The first area included a battery of questions, interspersed throughout the survey, that asked the respondents about the overall *value* they do or would expect to receive through membership in any association. These are referred to in the chapters as the *overarching value questions* (see box). The survey provided a definition for the term *association* that preceded and was referenced in the value questions, as follows:

> *Any scientific, scholarly, academic, or professional organization composed of individual members who seek to benefit from collective activities such as education, networking, or advocacy.*

Another question was also considered in the overarching value discussion but asked only of those who received the member version of the questionnaire. The question was based on the book *The Ultimate Question*, by Fred Reichheld (Harvard Business School Press, 2006): *"How likely is it that you would recommend membership [in a named organization] to a friend or colleague?"* This was asked on a scale from 0 to 10 and then recoded with a rating of 9 or 10 characterized as "promoter," 7 or 8 as "passive," and 6 or lower as "detractor." The thesis that Reichheld puts forth is that the best path to success for an organization is to increase the number of customers who are "promoters" by virtue of the fact that they answer the question with a strong affirmation. Conversely, organizations must reduce the number of customers who are "detractors" because they "sully" the organization's reputation as a consequence of their dissatisfaction.

In addition to these overarching value questions, respondents were asked if they had ever dropped their memberships in any association. For those who had, a list of possible reasons for dropping was provided for respondents to check, and an open field allowed them to provide the most compelling reasons.

Predisposition

The second line of questioning was designed to explore the notion of predisposition toward associations and also was asked of all respondents in reference to any association. Respondents selected from a list of nine generic association functions the three functions that they thought were the most important. The reader should be careful not to confuse these functions with a much more elaborate list of association "activities" that were addressed in the second part of the survey in reference to the sponsoring

association. Functions and activities are similar, but activities drill down much deeper.

Environmental Challenges

The third line of questioning about associations in general was intended to compensate for what was assumed to be wide variations in respondent familiarity with associations. A question was therefore developed to ask about the environmental challenges that concern professionals across fields and, without mentioning the connection to the role that most associations play in dealing with them. One need not be familiar with particular associations to be familiar with the challenges that affect association members. So in this series of questions, 16 challenges that appear in the environmental scans of many associations were presented, and respondents were asked to pick the three that they thought were most important. An open field was provided for respondents to add other challenges or customize those that were provided. Once they made their selection, respondents were then asked to evaluate the effectiveness of "associations" in addressing the three they selected.

One can see an implicit relationship between the list of association functions and the list of environmental challenges, though it is certainly not direct or comprehensive. It does provide an opportunity to expose one's disposition toward associations from a perspective of the type of functions they perform or challenges they address.

Environmental Challenges

Survey question:

Over the years, associations have identified some common challenges that concern professionals across fields. Some may not apply to your field. These challenges are summarized below. Please use the box to the left of each item to check the top three challenges that face your professional community.

- Inadequate recognition of the value delivered by your profession or discipline to the larger society
- Keeping up with new information in the field
- Keeping pace with technology
- Lack of public awareness of your field
- Inadequate sources of funding or revenue
- An expanding body of knowledge
- Inadequate supply of capable professionals
- Challenging regulatory environment (needed relief from regulations)
- Cost containment pressures
- Achieving high-quality outcomes
- Increasing competition (domestic or international)
- Rapidly changing, difficult-to-predict market conditions or trends
- Liability exposure, risk management
- Inadequate supply of support personnel
- Undesirable pending legislation
- Technology replacing practitioners

To Join or Not to Join a Particular Association

The second part of the study honed in on a specific decision to join or not. The two core questions in this part of the survey looked into the heart of the matter: What do I get? And how does this benefit my field or discipline? The first of these two questions refers to "personal benefits," and the second refers to the "good of the order." Each provided a list of specific program activities that are common to many but certainly not all associations. Each list was presented twice. In the first instance, all respondents, regardless of member or nonmember status, were asked to rate the inherent importance of each activity to their decision to join (using a five-point scale), and in the second presentation members were asked to rate their satisfaction with the association's performance (using a similar scale). Eight personal benefits and 12 good-of-the-order activities were provided.

Personal Benefits
("What do I get?")

Survey question to all respondents, regardless of member status:

How important were [would be] the following in your decision to join [a particular association]?

Survey question to members only:

How satisfied are you with the performance of this association in delivering benefits and services to you in the following areas?

- Access to the most up-to-date information available in your field
- Professional development or educational program offerings
- Opportunities for you to network with other professionals in your field
- Access to career information and employment opportunities
- Access to products, services, and suppliers (e.g. insurance, publications, etc.)
- Opportunities to gain leadership experience
- A reference directory of members/practitioners
- Member discounts or group purchasing activities

Gap Analysis

The difference between the mean scores for importance and performance were calculated to provide a metric on the performance gap perceived by members. A negative gap, where the mean score for importance exceeds that for performance, is considered a deficit that warrants attention. The urgency of the attention is a function of the activity's level of importance and the magnitude of the gap. Positive gaps mean performance exceeds importance. This is good if the activity is self sustaining. If it requires a subsidy from dues, it means the activity is consuming more valuable resources than is warranted. This method of performance measurement can be very productive when the survey is limited to a single association. In this survey, the offsetting effect of variations in the performance levels of 18 associations muted the gap measures to a point where they are referenced in only a few instances.

Segments: Demographics and Other Characteristics

The objective in segmenting a population for research of this type is to identify the characteristics that are most responsible for distinguishing needs that are unique to a subset of the membership and relate to a goal of the association. For example, members in an academic environment typically have unique needs that distinguish them from members in the private sector.

The following characteristics were identified in this survey and used to create the segments addressed throughout this report:

- Volunteer status: (covered along with member status in Chapter 4)
  - Yes or no to: *Have you volunteered in the last year? If yes:*
  - Governance (service on a parent or component board)
  - Programmatic activities (committee work)
  - Contribution through writing, speaking, or serving at events (ad hoc opportunities)
- Year of birth, used to create groups based on commonly accepted categories: (covered in Chapter 5)
  - Pre-War (age 60 or over)
  - Boomers (age 43 to 59)
  - Gen X (age 30 to 42)
  - Millennials (age under 30)
- Gender (Chapter 6)
- Employer type: (Chapter 7)
  - Private sector
  - Academic/educational
  - Nonprofit
  - Government
- Payment of dues: (also Chapter 7)
  - Self
  - Employer

- Country of residence used to create two subgroups inside and outside the United States. (Chapter 8)
    – United States residents
    – Outside United States
- (Note: Census profile data regarding race or ethnic group was requested, but the response rate to this question provided is insufficient for additional analysis.)

The Big Picture

The core questions of the survey, dealing with the respondents' attitudes toward associations in general, the challenges they face in their fields, and the importance of the benefits they receive or, in the case of nonmembers, that they could receive, as this related to the decision to join are summarized. The purpose of the chapter is simply to provide context for the more meaningful information that is generated by segmenting respondents into subsets that show significant differences in their perceptions of value, which is reported in subsequent chapters. Frequency tables for all respondents for all questions can be found in Appendix B.

THIS IS A STUDY of individuals. In addition to their relationship (or lack thereof) to one or more of the 18 co-sponsoring associations, the 16,944 respondents identified memberships in 5,200 other associations covering the gambit in scope from local to international, interest areas from aviation to zoology, and location from Abilene to Zimbabwe. We also received a large response from people who are not now members of any association, both among those who have been a member of one or more associations in the past and among those who have never been a member of any association.

This chapter provides highlights and data summaries from a big view that shows all of the responses in the aggregate for all questions asked in the study. Unless otherwise noted, the results reported in this chapter include all respondents regardless of member or nonmember status in any association now. Tables showing frequency of response to all questions can be found in Appendix B.

The purpose of this summary is to provide an orientation and context to the more useful information that is generated by the segment analyses and presented in subsequent chapters. The enormity of the database allowed considerable segmentation of respondents, and later chapters will cover demographic and behavioral characteristics in great detail.

The study began with a contextual definition of *association* for the purposes of the questions asked. This definition was needed to orient respondents to the distinction between an individual membership organization and trade associations, philanthropic groups, or fraternal organizations.

The term association *in all questions in this study refers to any scientific, scholarly, academic, or professional organization composed of individual members who seek to benefit from collective activities such as education, networking, or advocacy.*

Overarching Value Questions

The overarching value questions show that respondents are very favorably disposed toward associations and that the negatives about associations in general are extremely low.

EXHIBIT 3.1

What is your overall attitude toward associations as defined above?
(Rated on a scale of 1 to 5 with 5='Very Favorable')

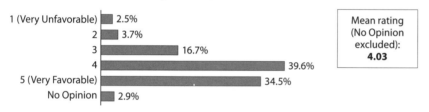

1 (Very Unfavorable)	2.5%
2	3.7%
3	16.7%
4	39.6%
5 (Very Favorable)	34.5%
No Opinion	2.9%

Mean rating (No Opinion excluded): **4.03**

EXHIBIT 3.2

Do you believe associations are capable of addressing the practical needs of individual members?
(Rated on a scale of 1 to 5 with 5='Definitely Yes')

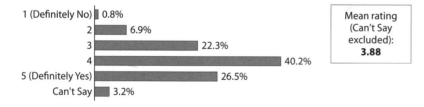

1 (Definitely No)	0.8%
2	6.9%
3	22.3%
4	40.2%
5 (Definitely Yes)	26.5%
Can't Say	3.2%

Mean rating (Can't Say excluded): **3.88**

EXHIBIT 3.3

Would you say there are too many associations in your professional area of interest, too few, or is the number about right?

Too Many	12.3%
Too Few	9.0%
About Right	63.0%
Can't Say	15.8%

EXHIBIT 3.4

Do you think there will be a greater or lesser need for associations five years from now?

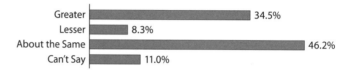

Greater	34.5%
Lesser	8.3%
About the Same	46.2%
Can't Say	11.0%

Functions of Associations

Eight functions that associations typically perform were listed in a question that asked respondents to pick the three that they thought were the most important. Exhibit B.3, shown in Appendix B, shows the frequency with which respondents selected each function. Each of the chapters observes how consistently the responses to this question aligned with those given by the various segments. The top five functions were

1. Providing training/professional development to members
2. Providing technical information to members
3. Providing timely information about the field to members
4. Connecting practitioners within a field to each other/networking
5. Creating and disseminating standards of practice

Environmental Challenges

Sixteen environmental challenges were identified, and respondents were again asked to identify the three that they thought were having the greatest impact on their field or profession. The question provided a redundant means of documenting the respondents' general impression of associations in that the issues that associations address provide a mirror image of the functions they perform. It this respect, it offers a cross check for association executives and managers to make sure that the functions that constitute their core capabilities align with the types of issues that are of the greatest concern to their members. This question also asked respondents to evaluate the effectiveness of associations in general in addressing the three issues they selected. This offered a third reference point on a cross comparison of issues, functions, and effectiveness. Exhibit 3.5 below provides a summary of these challenges.

EXHIBIT 3.5

Importance of Environmental Challenges

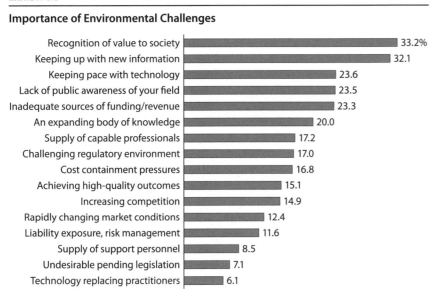

Recognition of value to society	33.2%
Keeping up with new information	32.1
Keeping pace with technology	23.6
Lack of public awareness of your field	23.5
Inadequate sources of funding/revenue	23.3
An expanding body of knowledge	20.0
Supply of capable professionals	17.2
Challenging regulatory environment	17.0
Cost containment pressures	16.8
Achieving high-quality outcomes	15.1
Increasing competition	14.9
Rapidly changing market conditions	12.4
Liability exposure, risk management	11.6
Supply of support personnel	8.5
Undesirable pending legislation	7.1
Technology replacing practitioners	6.1

Exhibit 3.6 below uses the second part of the challenges, where respondents were asked to evaluate the effectiveness of associations in dealing with these challenges, to make two points.

First, it makes a statement on the state of the art of association management, at least to the extent that this large and diverse population of people who are qualified to join an association (whether they do or not) see associations in general. The point is simply to illustrate an effective tool that individual associations could customize using challenges that more accurately reflect their environment. In the first two columns of the table, the frequency with which respondents selected the challenge was converted to

a rank order listing. The same conversion was made for the mean scores that respondents gave to the industry's effectiveness with respect to the challenge. The third column shows the difference between these two rank orderings. A negative difference represents an alarm point because it indicates that the significance of the challenge does not relate to the respondents' impression of the capability of the industry.

EXHIBIT 3.6

Rank Order of Challenges and Associations' Effectiveness in Meeting Them

	Challenge Rank	Association Effectiveness Rank	Degree of Difference
Inadequate recognition of the value delivered by the profession to the larger society	1	8	-7
Keeping up with new information in the field	2	1	1
Keeping pace with technology	3	3	0
Lack of public awareness of your field	4	12	-8
Inadequate sources of funding or revenue	5	16	-11
An expanding body of knowledge	6	2	4
Inadequate supply of capable professionals	7	13	-6
Challenging regulatory environment (needed relief from regulations)	8	6	2
Cost containment pressures	9	14	-5
Achieving high-quality outcomes	10	5	5
Increasing competition (domestic or international)	11	11	0
Rapidly changing, difficult to predict market conditions or trends	12	9	3
Liability exposure, risk management	13	10	3
Inadequate supply of support personnel	14	15	-1
Undesirable pending legislation	15	4	11
Technology replacing practitioners	16	7	9

Association managers have two options to consider in responding to any alarm point. One is to strengthen the capability of the association, and the other is make sure members understand the particular challenge is not relevant to the association's mission and therefore should not be a part of their expectations. Decisions like this are always made with some degree of risk. Running after issues that generate noise but are not relevant to the mission legitimizes the misplaced expectations and is not apt to be productive. On the other hand, ignoring issues that are critically important to members simply because the capability has not been developed—"we've never done anything like that before"—risks not being adequately adaptive in a changing environment.

To the extent that Exhibit 3.6 reflects respondents' current state of mind about associations, it indicates that the weak points of association management are perceived to be in its ability to affect public awareness, expand the availability of resources, and increase the supply of capable professionals. (See also Exhibit B.5 in Appendix B.)

Benefits

Both members and nonmembers of the co-sponsoring organization that contributed their names were asked to rate the importance of two types of benefits: "personal" and good-of-the-order benefits. In a follow-up question, members were asked to rate their satisfaction with the particular association's delivery. (See Exhibits B.9 and B.10 in Appendix B.)

Since this report is more concerned with associations in general than with any one association in particular, we report the average satisfaction ratings and gap analysis in the overall tables on these two questions but concentrate only on the importance question in most of the narrative.

Even though respondents answered questions in this part of the study in the context of a particular association, most associations offer some or all of the personal and good-of-the-order benefits described. Here are the Yin and the Yang of association management. The personal benefits make a compelling case for return on investment (ROI) reasons that an individual might use to justify membership. The good-of-the-order benefits to the field, on the other hand, raise the tides under everyone while giving a little boost to the social consciousness of the staff and volunteers who are responsible for delivering these benefits.

These complementary opposites work in tandem to propel the association management industry and give it its signature. The results of this study suggest that good-of-the-order benefits are more important to both people who are members of an association now and those who are not members now. The mean importance index for personal benefits is 3.4 versus a mean importance index of 3.6 for good-of-the-order benefits. While we try to clarify this value spectrum in this study, more research is needed to validate its importance to the intrinsic appeal of associating.

Demographic and Behavioral Characteristics

The most productive part of the study is found in the way the chapters show how demographic and behavioral characteristics affect responses to study questions. The answer to the question of how individuals determine value and why they choose to belong might lie in a quote attributed to an engineer: "In God we trust; everyone else should bring data." The data are here.

CHAPTER **4**

Affiliation and Involvement

Understandably, three segments—current members, former members, and those who have never held an association membership ("never" members)—value associations in varied ways. Understanding how is a crucial consideration, as is the unique value proposition of associations, which is the distinction between and combination of personal benefits, only available to members, and those that are directed toward "the good of the order." Equally important, we explore member involvement at four levels: governance volunteers, committee volunteers, single task (ad hoc) volunteers, and no involvement at all. Key findings include differences in the importance ratings that governing-level respondents give relative to all others, unique and possibly underappreciated attributes of ad hoc volunteers, and the fact that the uninvolved have some closer connections to former members than they do with those who are involved.

THE CLASSIC OBSERVATION THAT railroads stumbled when they failed to realize that they were in the transportation business, not railroading, represents the difference between knowing what you do versus knowing the utility you provide. One takes a producer-oriented view while the other takes a customer-oriented one. It's a matter of identity, and the questions that issue raises are important. Who are you and what utility do you offer?

The classic dilemma for many in the association business is the task of answering some version of that question. The government affairs person might say that he represents a community of interests. A publisher might say that she provides critical information to an industry or a profession. Professional development people might say that they facilitate learning opportunities in a given field. These highly varied answers may reflect the fact that the term *association* is a bit of an abstraction, so people start their responses by describing their particular medium. It also could be that like those railroaders who once stumbled, association professionals revert to a producer orientation because they don't quite understand their core business. This is easy to see in membership brochures that use bullets to describe the media that go into providing stuff to members. But where is the business of "associating" in all of that? There's networking; that's clearly a form of associating and typically one of the bullets. But it is worth noting that the other bullets are usually backed by committees and department heads, which gives them stature. Have you met many networking directors

Excerpt from Alexis de Tocqueville's
Of the Use which the Americans Make of Public Associations in Civil Life

THE AMERICANS MAKE ASSOCIATIONS to give entertainments, to found seminaries, to build inns, to construct churches, to diffuse books, to send missionaries to the antipodes; in this manner they found hospitals, prisons, and schools. If it is proposed to inculcate some truth or to foster some feeling by the encouragement of a great example, they form a society. Wherever at the head of some new undertaking you see the government in France, or a man of rank in England, in the United States you will be sure to find an association.

I have often admired the extreme skill with which the inhabitants of the United States succeed in proposing a common object for the exertions of a great many men and in inducing them voluntarily to pursue it.

Thus the most democratic country on the face of the earth is that in which men have, in our time, carried to the highest perfection the art of pursuing in common the object of their common desires and have applied this new science to the greatest number of purposes. Is this the result of accident, or is there in reality any necessary connection between the principle of association and that of equality?

It is easy to foresee that the time is drawing near when man will be less and less able to produce, by himself alone, the commonest necessaries of life. The task of the governing power will therefore perpetually increase, and its very efforts will extend it every day. The more it stands in the place of associations, the more will individuals, losing the notion of combining together, require its assistance: these are causes and effects that unceasingly create each other.

When the members of an aristocratic community adopt a new opinion or conceive a new sentiment, they give it a station, as it were, beside themselves, upon the lofty platform where they stand; and opinions or sentiments so conspicuous to the eyes of the multitude are easily introduced into the minds or hearts of all around. In democratic countries the governing power alone is naturally in a condition to act in this manner, but it is easy to see that its action is always inadequate, and often dangerous. A government can no more be competent to keep alive and to renew the circulation of opinions and feelings among a great people than to manage all the speculations of productive industry. No sooner does a government attempt to go beyond its political sphere and to enter upon this new track than it exercises, even unintentionally, an insupportable tyranny; for a government can only dictate strict rules, the opinions which it favors are rigidly enforced, and it is never easy to discriminate between its advice and its commands. Governments, therefore, should not be the only active powers; associations ought, in democratic nations, to stand in lieu of those powerful private individuals whom the equality of conditions has swept away.

As soon as several of the inhabitants of the United States have taken up an opinion or a feeling which they wish to promote in the world, they look out for mutual assistance; and as soon as they have found one another out, they combine. From that moment they are no longer isolated men, but a power seen from afar, whose actions serve for an example and whose language is listened to.

Nothing, in my opinion, is more deserving of our attention than the intellectual and moral associations of America. The political and industrial associations of that country strike us forcibly; but the others elude our observation, or if we discover them, we understand them imperfectly because we have hardly ever seen anything of the kind. It must be acknowledged, however, that they are as necessary to the American people as the former, and perhaps more so. In democratic countries the science of association is the mother of science; the progress of all the rest depends upon the progress it has made.

Among the laws that rule human societies there is one which seems to be more precise and clear than all others. If men are to remain civilized or to become so, the art of associating together must grow and improve in the same ratio in which the equality of conditions is increased.

lately? Could it be that associating has become merely a byproduct of what associations are so busy doing?

If at this point you feel any discomfort with understanding the utility that associations offer, shift your attention momentarily to the sidebar that provides excerpts from the analysis Alexis de Tocqueville did of American associations, starting back in the 1830s. He laid the entire destiny of democracy at the feet of associations and sums it up by saying:

> *Among the laws that rule human societies there is one which seems to be more precise and clear than all others. If men are to remain civilized or to become so, the art of associating together must grow and improve in the same ratio in which the equality of conditions is increased.*

After reading the sidebar, or better yet, after visiting the Web site (www.tocqueville.org) and reading the entire chapter, practitioners of this "art of associating" might ask themselves one not-so-simple question: How is it that an 19th-century tourist, while merely visiting the United States, not only stumbles upon associations but goes on to write an intellectually profound and enduring explanation of democracy in which he cites associations as being the critical catalyst necessary to sustain liberty; and yet 150 years later many association managers appear to be missing the Frenchman's insights as evidenced by their own marketing materials?

A contemporary effort to understand associations might entail looking at them as cooperatives, or "co-ops," which are venues through which people come together to exchange things like information and initiatives. Associations may comprise the only industry that has as its primary suppliers the very same database of people who receive benefits as the main customers. Other suppliers might come to mind, like hospitality and printing, but with all due respect, they are secondary suppliers. Members submit papers, give presentations, answer questions, share experiences, and provide their energy, all in the context of a black box that receives, sorts, analyzes, supplements, and recompiles everything in a way that makes value-added information and initiatives accessible to the very same population that gave it in fragments. Members are suppliers and customers. Information and initiative are the inputs and the outputs. The activity of giving and receiving is a function of their willingness to associate. Secondary suppliers facilitate important processes, and other customers certainly benefit, but

this unique input-output cycle is the engine that drives the system. At their core, associations are built on a give-to-get business proposition. Not every getter is a giver, but the ratio is strong enough to keep the system moving. The marketing materials that many associations use to describe the value they deliver fail to reflect this co-op mentality or the shared vision of the values that fuel the system.

This chapter looks first at the decision to affiliate with others in a common cause and then at the factors that motivate them to be givers as opposed to sitting back as getters. The survey findings indicate that understanding the idea of common cause and the motivation of givers is the heart of the matter and the key to success.

Affiliation

The decision to join is more accurately a decision to affiliate. The term *join* implies jumping in, like a party in a pool. *Affiliate* means more than that. It incorporates the notion of shared identity. When people affiliate, they let the world around them know that they share an important quality with this group. It is not so much a purchase as it is an exchange, the content of which starts with identity but involves a shared commitment to some common purpose, an end game that warrants collaboration. Peter Drucker notes that there are three types of organizations, and they are fundamentally different in terms of motivating drivers:

- For-profits are driven by the prospects of return-on-investment.
- Governments are about providing public services from taxes.
- Associations are about advancing a cause based on a common vision and shared values.

This study tries to establish a baseline understanding of the factors that individuals analyze as they consider affiliating with a particular association. But before moving in that close, the study backed off to consider the decision maker's predisposition toward associations in general. The response to the survey was large enough to isolate three populations in this pre-decision phase, one of which constitutes a portion of the United States population that is so small that this may be the first time association researchers have had the opportunity to investigate them on this scale.

Three Fundamental Segments

The three segments of the respondent population under consideration here may require a slight reorientation in the way association professionals tend to dichotomize their world into "members" and "nonmembers." This survey aggregated lists of members and nonmembers from 18 associations and asked a series of questions about their current and former affiliations with *any* association. This information allows segmenting in a way that breaks the standard dichotomy of members and nonmembers into three distinct populations:

- Current members of one or more associations
- People who are not currently members of any association, but are former members of at least one (nonmembers with association experience)
- People who have never been members of any association and are referred to here as "never" members (non-joiners, at least to this point in their lives)

Exhibit 4.1 shows how respondents from co-sponsoring associations and respondents from any association break down in this study.

EXHIBIT 4.1

Member Status—Any Association and Co-sponsor Association Status Compared

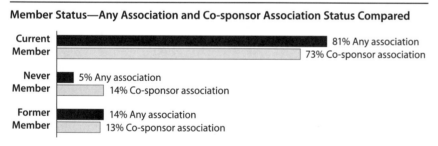

The enormity of the response database provides a large enough sampling to isolate "never" members and compare them reliably with the other two categories. This is significant because, as Tocqueville accurately noted, the United States is a nation of pluralists who get things done through voluntary groups that form and disband as need dictates. Finding a large enough population of American adults who are not joiners, or who have not yet joined an association is a challenge that this survey overcame through

sheer numbers. This three-segment comparison is limited to the preliminary questions about associations in general because the "never" group of non-joiners was not qualified to answer the specific phase-two questions about a specific association experience.

Affiliations in General

Asked about their attitude toward associations in general, 37 percent of the current members give it the highest rating on a five-point scale, which is a very positive evaluation. Former members and those who have never been members of any association each give nearly the same "very favorable" ratings—10 percentage points lower than those of current members. All three populations were nearly identical in terms of the percentage that indicates a "very unfavorable" attitude. If this were politics, voter attitudes toward associations would be said to carry strong favorable ratings with very low "negatives," which is excellent field position because negatives are barriers that must be removed before positive messages have a chance of getting through (Exhibit 4.2).

When the questioning moves to the more discerning matter of whether or not they believe associations "are capable of addressing the practical needs of individual members," the percentage giving the most positive rating drops substantially for current members. While differences among the three populations on this question may seem modest, they are statistically significant, and that raises two noteworthy points. First, being "capable of addressing the practical needs" of the members is one of the fundamental assumptions that underlies the decision to join. That "never" members are fairly close to current members on this means that the marketing challenge of moving them into the fold should be reasonably attainable. It further substantiates the favorable position that associations seem to have. The second point is that, on this question, former members are as far from "never" members as never members are from current members. This introduces a theme that is reinforced throughout the survey findings. One disappointing association experience casts a negative shadow over future invitations to join. In other words, a former member of one association who has not joined another association is, by virtue of that experience, harder for any other association to recruit.

EXHIBIT 4.2

Overarching Value Questions by Individual Member Status
(All are significantly different.*)

	Current Member	Never Member	Former Member
What is your overall attitude toward associations? *(5-point scale, 5='very favorable')*			
Mean	4.06	3.92	3.85
(% 'very favorable')	37.0%	28.7%	27.3%
Do you believe associations are capable of addressing the practical needs of individual members? *(5-point scale, 5='definitely yes')*			
Mean	3.91	3.81	3.68
(% 'definitely yes')	28.4%	25.3%	21.8%
Would you say that there are too many associations in your professional area of interest, too few, or is the number about right?			
Too many	14.9%	14.8%	13.6%
Too few	9.1%	19.9%	16.1%
About right	76.0%	65.4%	70.3%
Do you think there will be a greater or lesser need for associations five years from now?			
Greater	38.0%	49.8%	37.2%
Lesser	9.0%	8.6%	12.6%
About the same	53.0%	41.5%	50.2%

Those who are members of an association now are more likely than others to give the highest rating (5) to associations as defined in the questionnaire, but when the mean rating on the 1-5 scale is calculated, all respondents are close regardless of current member status. Current members are more likely than others to think there are the right number of associations serving their professional interest area and to believe that the need for associations will be about the same in the next five years.

* "Significant" differences in this and all tables refers to a finding of statistically significant differences based on the application of an appropriate statistical test.

Functions of an Association

In the search for factors that differentiate the way these three populations discern value with respect to the decision to join an association, it is useful to first note how they are the same (Exhibit 4.3). Networking, technical information, and professional development are among the most important association functions to all segments studied, and these three populations reflect that shared perception, showing no significant differences in the incidence of selecting these factors as most important. Five of the nine generic association functions did show how the groups differ significantly. (See Chapter 2 for a complete list of functions.)

- "Timely information about the field" was less frequently deemed an important function among former members than it was among current or never members, both of whom share a similar and much higher estimation.

- Former members were more likely to select "creating and disseminating standards of practice," and this is the only function that they are more likely to select than others.

- Current members select government affairs and public affairs more frequently than either of the other groups do, with "never" members distinguishing themselves by selecting this much less frequently.

- Certification is the only function that current members select less frequently than do the other two groups.

Challenges Facing the Profession

Respondents were given a list of 16 generic environmental challenges that many professions face and were asked to select three that they believe to be among the most important. They were then asked to rate the effectiveness of associations in dealing with their top three challenges. The six challenges listed in bold in Exhibit 4.4 are the ones for which the three populations show significant differences in their responses.

From this the following observations can be made:

- Never members are less likely to be concerned with recognition of the profession in the larger society.

- Former members are less likely to be concerned about keeping up with an expanding body of knowledge.
- Never members are more likely to be concerned with an inadequate supply of capable professionals.
- Never members are less likely to be concerned with a challenging regulatory environment.
- Never members are more likely to be concerned with achieving high-quality outcomes.
- Never members are less likely to be concerned with issues having to do with pending legislation.

EXHIBIT 4.3

What do you think are the most important functions of an association?
(Respondents selected up to 3 choices. Significant differences in bold.)

	Current Member		Never Member		Former Member	
	%	Rank	%	Rank	%	Rank
Providing training/professional development to members	46.2%	1	48.7%	1	47.1%	1
Providing technical information to members	43.9%	2	41.4%	2	41.5%	2
Providing timely information about the field to members	**37.3%**	**3**	**38.4%**	**3**	**33.9%**	**4**
Connecting practitioners within the field to each other/networking	36.6%	4	36.3%	4	36.4%	3
Creating and disseminating standards of practice	**30.6%**	**5**	**27.7%**	**5**	**33.6%**	**5**
Representing the field to the government	**28.2%**	**6**	**19.5%**	**9**	**24.3%**	**7**
Representing the field to the public	**27.6%**	**7**	**23.2%**	**7**	**25.0%**	**6**
Representing the field within the industry or discipline	20.4%	8	22.7%	8	20.8%	9
Providing certification opportunities	**18.7%**	**9**	**24.8%**	**6**	**22.4%**	**8**

Frequency of choosing (%) and priority (rank) are similar regardless of member status for the five highest-ranked items. There is wide variation by member status in both frequency and rank for "Representing the field to the government," which is a low priority among those who have never been a member of an association in the past.

Percent % shows the frequency the item was checked by each type of respondent. Rank is the order of priority. "Significant" differences in this and all tables refers to a finding of statistically significant differences based on the application of an appropriate statistical test.

EXHIBIT 4.4

Select the top three challenges that face your professional community.
(Respondents selected up to 3 choices. Significant differences in bold.)

	Current Member		Never Member		Former Member	
	%	Rank	%	Rank	%	Rank
Inadequate recognition of the value delivered by the profession or discipline to the larger society	**34.2%**	**1**	**23.6%**	**4**	**32.7%**	**1**
Keeping up with new information in the field	32.8%	2	29.9%	1	30.2%	2
Lack of public awareness of your field	23.3%	3	20.0%	7	24.8%	4
Inadequate sources of funding or revenue	23.3%	4	25.7%	2	21.7%	5
Keeping pace with technology	23.3%	5	24.3%	3	24.9%	3
An expanding body of knowledge	**20.5%**	**6**	**20.1%**	**6**	**16.7%**	**7**
Challenging regulatory environment (needed relief from regulations)	**17.6%**	**7**	**13.2%**	**11**	**16.5%**	**8**
Inadequate supply of capable professionals	**17.5%**	**8**	**20.4%**	**5**	**15.2%**	**9**
Cost containment pressures	16.2%	9	19.1%	9	18.7%	6
Achieving high-quality outcomes	**14.8%**	**10**	**19.6%**	**8**	**14.9%**	**11**
Increasing competition (domestic or international)	14.5%	11	18.5%	10	15.2%	10
Rapidly changing, difficult to predict market conditions or trends	12.2%	12	11.0%	13	13.9%	12
Liability exposure, risk management	11.6%	13	12.4%	12	11.4%	13
Inadequate supply of support personnel	8.4%	14	10.2%	14	8.6%	14
Undesirable pending legislation	**7.2%**	**15**	**3.8%**	**16**	**8.0%**	**15**
Technology replacing practitioners	5.9%	16	5.7%	15	6.6%	16

"Inadequate recognition of the value delivered by the profession or discipline" and "Lack of public awareness of your field," two related concepts, are more important to those who are now or have been members of an association in the past than it is to those who have never been a member. "Keeping up with new information in the field" is of high importance across the board.

Percent % shows the frequency the item was checked by each type of respondent. Rank is the order of priority. "Significant" differences in this and all tables refers to a finding of statistically significant differences based on the application of an appropriate statistical test.

Preferred Means of Receiving Information

Respondents were asked to identify their preferred means of receiving information about their field by selecting up to three choices from a list of 12 media (Exhibit 4.5). Three modes of delivery were significant in differentiating respondents by membership status. Though none of them are surprising, they are worth noting. Those who worry about member retention are frequently heard to say that "the only thing many members are aware of getting from us is the magazine." This may be true, but it doesn't degrade the value of a magazine or journal. This is one of the few areas in which former members give a higher value rating than never members, which speaks to the fundamental value that former members associate with such publications even after they leave the membership.

Conferences or meetings are more important to current members, but unlike the magazine or journal, which is usually included with dues, this preference may reflect the ability to afford participation. That never members show a higher preference for the Internet may reflect the fact that this population tends to be younger, but the analysis of generations and career stages indicates that use of the Internet no longer reflects that great an age bias (refer to Exhibit 5.8 for more information). It may then be equally true that nonmembers work this medium harder than do current members simply to compensate for the absence of the steady flow of information that goes to current members.

EXHIBIT 4.5

How do you prefer to receive information about your profession or field?
(Respondents selected up to 3 choices. Significant differences in bold.)

	Current Member		Never Member		Former Member	
	%	Rank	%	Rank	%	Rank
In magazines or journals serving your field	**65.5%**	**1**	**55.5%**	**1**	**57.8%**	**1**
At Conferences or meetings	**54.5%**	**2**	**50.0%**	**2**	**47.3%**	**4**
In E-newsletters	52.9%	3	48.8%	3	51.0%	2
Through an association Web site	47.2%	4	46.9%	4	49.1%	3
By searching on the Internet	**16.7%**	**5**	**24.9%**	**5**	**18.9%**	**5**
Through your network of peers (word of mouth)	12.2%	6	12.3%	6	13.6%	6
Through communities of practice (e.g. special interest groups, user groups, etc.)	11.9%	7	11.6%	7	12.1%	7
In print sources other than magazines or newspapers	6.5%	8	7.3%	8	7.2%	8
In general interest magazines	3.9%	9	6.0%	9	3.9%	9
In newspapers (print)	3.2%	10	3.5%	10	3.3%	10
Through blogs or podcasts	2.0%	11	1.7%	12	2.3%	12
Through traditional broadcast media (television or radio)	1.7%	12	2.3%	11	2.5%	11

Few differences are found in preferences for delivery of information about the respondent's profession or field, although magazines or journals (usually the most valued member benefit) are more strongly preferred by members. Searching on the Internet is more frequently preferred by never members.

Percent % shows the frequency the item was checked by each type of respondent. Rank is the order of priority. "Significant" differences in this and all tables refers to a finding of statistically significant differences based on the application of an appropriate statistical test.

Reasons for Dropping

To understand how current and former members might differ when it comes to dropping membership in an association, all respondents, regardless of membership status with the organization that supplied their names, were asked if they had ever dropped membership in any association (Exhibit 4.6). (It is worth noting that nearly half of the current members reported having dropped some association membership in the past.) The survey laid out 14 possible reasons for dropping and offered an open-ended option for the respondents to add others (Exhibit 4.6a). An analysis of the open responses identified little other than variations on the list of reasons that was provided.

As one might expect, the failure to deliver the expected value is by far the most prevalent reason for dropping a membership. But two of the more extreme differentiators have to do with interpersonal fit and the purely economic matter of who pays the dues. That "the group was not right for me" may need closer inspection in future surveys, as it could mean either a lack of hospitality offered or fundamental differences in identity, as in "they are not like me." But those who give this reason are less likely to give up on associations entirely, since they are members of some association now.

Anyone who has surveyed former members to find out why they dropped their membership is familiar with and probably frustrated by the value-cost reason, which is easy to understand on the surface, yet offers no remedial information. For most people, expectations are a direct function of cost. For some, like those whose dues are paid by their employers, cost may be a less pressing factor, but responsible people nevertheless maintain this as a key part of the decision making. To probe this reason for a deeper understanding of what it does and does not include, the 14 reasons were sorted into categories having to do with reasons that are either within or outside an association's control.

When considered in this way, one half of those who are currently members who have dropped membership in an association in the past did so for reasons having to do with that association's performance (Exhibit 4.6b). The bad news is that associations are, on average, responsible for half of their drops. And although it may not be good news, this certainly should offer some level of relief to those who fret over retention figures. One half of the respondents who are current members of a sponsoring association and who have dropped membership in some other organization report that they did so for reasons that were outside that association's control. Former members are either less scrutinizing of the associations they belong to or more apt to change career direction. While 45 percent of them report dropping an association membership for reasons that relate to the association's performance, the majority cite reasons beyond the association's control.

EXHIBIT 4.6

Have you ever dropped membership in any association?

	Current member	Never Member	Former Member
% Yes	50.2	0	100

EXHIBIT 4.6a

[Asked only if respondent ever dropped membership in any association. By definition, this excludes those who have never been members of any association.] **Did any of the following play a role in your decision to drop membership in the association you dropped most recently?**
(Respondents selected up to five choices. Significant differences in bold.)

	Current Member		Former Member	
	%	Rank	%	Rank
Did not receive the expected value to justify the cost of dues	55.7%	1	57.2%	1
Employer stopped paying membership dues	**15.6%**	**9**	**27.0%**	**2**
Change of career focus	26.3%	2	23.6%	3
Not enough local programs offered*	16.5%	7	19.6%	4
Change of job	16.6%	6	18.4%	5
Dissatisfied with association performance*	**21.9%**	**3**	**16.9%**	**6**
Change of professional interest	**21.5%**	**4**	**16.3%**	**7**
Association was ineffective in representing your field*	**18.3%**	**5**	**14.4%**	**8**
Dissatisfied with the local chapter*	9.6%	11	9.6%	9
The group was not the right one for me	**15.8%**	**8**	**8.4%**	**10**
Change of residence	8.7%	12	8.1%	11
Disagreed with association's political/advocacy positions*	9.8%	10	7.1%	12
Did not feel welcomed in the group*	6.3%	13	5.8%	13
Change of local chapter relationship with association*	2.5%	14	2.0%	14

Percent % shows the frequency the item was checked by each type of respondent. Rank is the order of priority. "Significant" differences in this and all tables refers to a finding of statistically significant differences based on the application of an appropriate statistical test.
* See note for Exhibit 4.6b.

EXHIBIT 4.6b

Reason for dropping having to do with an association's performance

	Current Member	Former Member
% Yes	50.3%	45.0%

A new variable was created based on respondents who reported having dropped any association in the past who checked one or more of the reasons designated with an * in Exhibit 4.6a. The results are shown in Exhibit 4.6b.

Demographic Differences

Several other differences are worth posting but warrant little commentary, either because they speak for themselves or are not explained by other findings:

- Never members are less apt to be found in the private sector (Exhibit 4.7).
- Never members are more likely to be found in the entry-level positions. (This is also a function of age; see Chapter 5, "Generations and Career Level.") (Exhibit 4.9)
- Former members are more likely to be females. (See Chapter 6, "Gender.") (Exhibit 4.10)
- Former members are more likely to be employed by organizations that don't pay dues and never members are less likely to know, probably because they have not asked (Exhibit 4.8).

EXHIBIT 4.7

Which of the following best describes the type of organization in which you are employed?

	Current Member	Never Member	Former Member
Private sector	49.4%	40.3%	53.6%
Academia/education	27.1%	28.5%	17.0%
Nonprofit	13.0%	18.4%	18.2%
Government	10.6%	12.7%	11.2%

EXHIBIT 4.8

Does employer pay dues?
(Employed respondents were asked this question regardless of current member status in any association.)

	Current Member	Never Member	Former Member
Yes	49.9%	17.2%	24.7%
No	48.4%	56.0%	64.2%
Don't know	*1.7%**	*26.8%*	*11.0%*

* Current members might not know if their employer would pay because they pay themselves and have not asked.

EXHIBIT 4.9

Which best describes your current career situation?
(Excludes academia, unemployed, self employed, and retired)

	Current Member	Never Member	Former Member
Entry level	5.5%	14.4%	6.5%
Mid level	46.4%	57.3%	54.7%
Senior level but not CEO	42.2%	25.2%	33.8%
Chief Executive	5.8%	3.2%	5.1%

EXHIBIT 4.10

What is your gender?

	Current Member	Never Member	Former Member
Male	55.5%	53.4%	48.8%
Female	44.5%	46.6%	51.2%

Involvement, the Key to Maintaining Affiliation

The impact that voluntary service has on the perception of value was looked into by segmenting three groups based on levels of involvement and a fourth for those who were not involved. Predictably, respondents' perception of value from the association increases with their level of involvement (Exhibit 4.11). The segments are

- Governance volunteers: those who reported serving on the national or local board for the organization in the last year
- Committee volunteers: those who reported serving on any type of committee in the last year
- Ad hoc volunteers: those who participated in the value-adding work of the association by performing at least one quantifiable task, as opposed to the extended (and often uncertain) commitment of a committee in the last year
- Nonparticipants: those who have not served in the last year

EXHIBIT 4.11

Volunteer Activity for an Association in the Last 12 Months

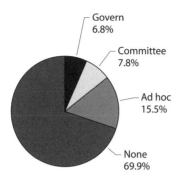

Govern
6.8%

Committee
7.8%

Ad hoc
15.5%

None
69.9%

Three value questions that probe the respondents' attitude toward associations in general and the "ultimate" question that asks if they would put their reputation on the line by recommending membership in the sponsoring association all create a positive impression that line up clearly with one's level of involvement. The more involved a person is with a particular association, the more positive the rating becomes for associations in general and the more likely they are to be a promoter for the particular organization (Exhibits 4.12 and 4.13).

By way of comparison, the "very favorable" ratings for never and former members on the overall attitude toward associations is 28.7 percent and 27.3 percent respectively; and for "addressing the practical needs" it was 25.3 percent and 21.8 percent (see Exhibit 4.2).

It is worth noting that the never member rating on the "addressing the practical needs" question was a mere 2 percent below that of current members with no involvement. Is this good or bad? It's good if one thinks that it means the never members need only a nudge to bring them into the fold. It's bad if one thinks that members with no involvement are two points way from nonmembers who associate less value with the larger scale, good-of-the-order activities like government affairs and public awareness. The greatest concern reflected in this table is seen in the range of difference between the most and least involved on The Ultimate Question. Word of mouth from a colleague is the number one way current members come to know about the association and the opportunity to join (see Exhibit B.11 in Appendix B). The Ultimate Question—*Would you recommend the*

association to a colleague?—is the number one recruitment vehicle at an association's disposal, and any level of involvement is the marketing catapult that can make a real difference.

EXHIBIT 4.12

Overarching Value Questions by Individual Volunteer Activity
(Current members only. Significant differences in bold.)

	Governance	Committee	None
What is your overall attitude toward associations? *(5-point scale, 5='very favorable')*			
Mean	**4.26**	**4.26**	**4.05**
(% 'very favorable')	**50.7%**	**47.0%**	**35.8%**
Do you believe associations are capable of addressing the practical needs of individual members? *(5-point scale, 5= 'definitely yes')*			
Mean	**4.16**	**4.15**	**3.90**
(% 'definitely yes')	**40.6%**	**37.3%**	**27.2%**
Would you say that there are too many associations in your professional area of interest, too few, or is the number about right?			
Too many	17.6%	16.6%	13.3%
Too few	6.1%	6.2%	8.5%
About right	76.4%	77.2%	78.2%
Do you think there will be a greater or lesser need for associations five years from now?			
Greater	39.7	36.7	37.2
Lesser	11.8	11.3	8.2
About the same	48.5	52.0	54.5

Responses to the first two of these questions are clearly affected by level of volunteer activity. The greater the level of activity the higher the probability of rating at the extreme (5). Things even out at the mean once the respondent is involved on the committee or higher level.

"Significant" differences in this and all tables refers to a finding of statistically significant differences based on the application of an appropriate statistical test.

EXHIBIT 4.13

How likely is it that you would recommend membership in *[a particular association]* to a friend or colleague?

(Asked only of current members about a particular association. 10-point scale summarized. See The Ultimate Question *by Fred Reichheld.)*

	Governance	Committee	Ad hoc	None
Promoter (rating 9 or 10)	65.8%	60.7%	46.8%	39.6%
Passive (rating 7 or 8)	21.7%	27.2%	33.6%	31.8%
Detractor (rating 6 or lower)	12.5%	12.1%	19.6%	28.6%
	100.0%	100.0%	100.0%	100.0%

These differences are significant and clearly reflect the level of volunteer involvement.

Functions

Exhibit 4.14 shows the rank order of importance that each segment reports for the generic functions of an association. There are three significant differences:

- Ad hoc volunteers put the highest importance on networking, whereas all others put it on professional development. The implication may be that single tasks are the fast track to networking. Networking is a personal benefit. Committee assignments involve considerably more work and therefore may require more allegiance to motivations having to do with the good of the order.

- People who report no involvement place less importance on networking. Is that because they simply don't value it or have not been made aware of the value it offers?

- People with no involvement place greater importance on creating and disseminating standards of practice, an attribute that also distinguishes former members from never members. (See Exhibit 4.3.)

EXHIBIT 4.14

What do you think are the most important functions of an association?

(Respondents selected up to 3 choices. Significant differences in bold.)

	Governance		Committee		Ad hoc		None	
	%	Rank	%	Rank	%	Rank	%	Rank
Providing training/professional development to members	**47.8%**	**1**	**45.1%**	**1**	**31.4%**	**6**	**48.1%**	**1**
Connecting practitioners within the field to each other/networking	**42.9%**	**2**	**39.8%**	**2**	**46.6%**	**1**	**33.4%**	**4**
Providing technical information to members	39.4%	3	39.6%	3	41.1%	2	46.4%	2
Providing timely information about the field to members	35.0%	4	31.7%	6	39.5%	3	35.8%	3
Representing the field to the public	32.2%	5	33.1%	5	39.0%	4	26.1%	7
Representing the field to the government	30.9%	6	33.2%	4	33.8%	5	28.2%	6
Creating and disseminating standards of practice	**27.9%**	**7**	**29.8%**	**7**	**25.7%**	**7**	**33.0%**	**5**
Representing the field within the industry or discipline	20.4%	8	22.1%	8	18.6%	8	20.9%	8
Providing certification opportunities	17.8%	9	17.9%	9	11.6%	9	20.5%	9

People who volunteer on an ad hoc basis are less likely to see training/professional development as an important function for an association. This may have to do with the high incidence of 'ad hoc' volunteers outside the United States (See Exhibit 8.7). The high priority ad hoc volunteers place on networking suggests that networking might be the ultimate "what's in it for me" for ad hoc volunteers.

Percent % shows the frequency the item was checked by each type of respondent. Rank is the order of priority. "Significant" differences in this and all tables refers to a finding of statistically significant differences based on the application of an appropriate statistical test.

Challenges

Twelve of the 16 environmental challenges show significant differences by level of involvement. As seen in Exhibit 4.15, all four groups rank "inadequate recognition of the value delivered by the profession or discipline to the larger society" as their number one concern, but they do so with different levels of adamancy. The difference between this challenge and the "lack of public awareness of your field" challenge that ranks second for the more involved and fourth for the less or uninvolved is that one is about recognizing the field at all; the other is about having an accurate understanding of the value that is delivered. The decline in importance for this challenge ramps down with the level of involvement and extends further to include never and former members but on a far lower level of magnitude.

EXHIBIT 4.15

Select the top three challenges that face your professional community.
(Respondents selected up to 3 choices. Significant differences in bold.)

	Governance		Committee		Ad hoc		None	
	%	Rank	%	Rank	%	Rank	%	Rank
Inadequate recognition of the value delivered by the profession or discipline to the larger society	**42.5%**	**1**	**44.0%**	**1**	**37.2%**	**1**	**35.8%**	**1**
Lack of public awareness of your field	**35.3%**	**2**	**32.0%**	**2**	**27.1%**	**4**	**23.7%**	**4**
Keeping up with new information in the field	**28.3%**	**3**	**30.7%**	**3**	**32.7%**	**3**	**32.8%**	**2**
Inadequate sources of funding or revenue	**22.7%**	**4**	**23.2%**	**4**	**37.2%**	**2**	**20.2%**	**5**
Inadequate supply of capable professionals	**21.1%**	**5**	**17.9%**	**7**	**14.9%**	**8**	**18.2%**	**7**
Keeping pace with technology	**19.9%**	**6**	**21.6%**	**6**	**17.6%**	**6**	**26.1%**	**3**
An expanding body of knowledge	**19.3%**	**7**	**22.4%**	**5**	**23.9%**	**5**	**18.9%**	**6**
Challenging regulatory environment (needed relief from regulations)	**18.3%**	**8**	**17.8%**	**8**	**11.3%**	**11**	**17.5%**	**8**
Cost containment pressures	14.8%	9	14.8%	9	14.0%	9	16.1%	9
Increasing competition (domestic or international)	14.6%	10	12.4%	11	13.9%	10	15.1%	10
Rapidly changing, difficult to predict market conditions or trends	**12.0%**	**11**	**10.9%**	**12**	**9.0%**	**12**	**12.3%**	**13**
Liability exposure, risk management	**9.5%**	**12**	**9.2%**	**13**	**7.0%**	**14**	**13.1%**	**12**
Inadequate supply of support personnel	8.6%	13	8.5%	14	8.3%	13	8.1%	14
Achieving high-quality outcomes	**8.6%**	**14**	**12.8%**	**10**	**15.6%**	**7**	**13.6%**	**11**
Undesirable pending legislation	8.4%	15	7.2%	15	6.7%	15	7.2%	15
Technology replacing practitioners	**7.7%**	**16**	**4.8%**	**16**	**4.0%**	**16**	**6.4%**	**16**

While there are variations in the intensity (%), there seems to be agreement (rank) that the number one challenge is "Inadequate recognition of the value delivered by the profession or discipline on the larger society." Associations would do well to either address this issue or educate their stakeholders about why it is outside their mission.

Percent % shows the frequency the item was checked by each type of respondent. Rank is the order of priority. "Significant" differences in this and all tables refers to a finding of statistically significant differences based on the application of an appropriate statistical test.

Other observations on these differences include:

- "Inadequate supply of capable professionals" is a challenge that governance volunteers think is more important than do others. This introduces an observation that is seen more clearly in the findings on benefits to the field (see Exhibit 4.17). That is, in responding to some of these questions, leaders appear to take on a collective point of view that reflects a sense of responsibility for the good of the order.

- Keeping pace with technology is a more critical challenge for those who are not involved. This may reflect their lower level of concern for the larger social challenges; or they may be less involved because the technological rate of change in their environment is more demanding.

- Achieving high-quality outcomes is more important to those who perform limited tasks. This could possibly connect with the emphasis they place on networking in that it may point to the kind of information they seek for that activity.

Personal Benefits

Personal benefits that serve individual needs are summarized in Exhibit 4.16. It raises one of the few inconsistencies between a segment's responses to the question on association functions in general and the similar but more specific questions on benefits delivered by a particular association. The segment that is involved with ad hoc volunteering reported networking as the most important function of an association and here, as a personal benefit, it ranks second. In both questions, there was consistency in their top three selections, so the variance may simply be an anomaly. With respect to networking, the value it is perceived as having clearly escalates with involvement, which raises the chicken-and-egg question: Does more involvement raise one's awareness of the value of networking, or do those who value networking rise more readily to the more highly involved leadership positions?

The answer to this question might be partially reflected in the observation that the ad hoc volunteer segment and the uninvolved both rate

EXHIBIT 4.16

How IMPORTANT were [would be] the following personal benefits in your decision to join?
(Rated on 1-5 scale with 5=very important. Mean rating shown. Asked about a particular association to both members and nonmembers. Significant differences in bold.)

	Governance		Committee		Ad hoc		None	
	Mean	Rank	Mean	Rank	Mean	Rank	Mean	Rank
Opportunities for you to network with other professionals in your field	4.29	1	4.24	1	3.94	2	3.61	3
Access to the most up to date information available in your field	4.22	2	4.22	2	4.21	1	4.21	1
Professional development or educational program offerings	4.20	3	4.08	3	3.55	3	3.96	2
Opportunities to gain leadership experience	3.62	4	3.50	4	2.83	6	2.84	7
Access to career information and employment opportunities	3.26	5	3.47	5	3.28	4	3.37	4
Access to products, services, and suppliers	3.14	6	3.07	7	3.14	5	3.15	5
A reference directory of members/practitioners	3.08	7	3.08	6	2.78	7	2.87	6
Member discounts or group purchasing activities	2.54	8	2.41	8	2.61	8	2.67	8

While respondents answered these questions in reference to a particular association, most associations offer some or all of the personal benefits listed here. There are clear differences in priority (rank) by volunteer level, although governance- and committee-level volunteers prioritize the importance of these items similarly. Ad hoc volunteers and those who don't volunteer at all diverge, particularly on the issue of opportunities for gaining leadership experience.

Mean shows the average rating on a 1-5 scale with 5=very important. Rank is the order of priority. "Significant" differences in this and all tables refers to a finding of statistically significant differences based on the application of an appropriate statistical test.

"opportunities to gain leadership" lower than the more involved. The rank order of these two benefits for everyone may indicate that while all segments value networking, those who actually do it through their involvement come to value it more highly and, as a consequence, develop greater appreciation for the value of leadership experience.

Benefits to Field: "The Good of the Order"

The most notable difference with respect to good-of-the-order benefits by level of involvement has to do with the struggles that take place among various interest groups that might be expected to work collaboratively but face challenges in doing it. Leaders at the governing level rate "promoting a greater appreciation of the role and value of the field among practitioners" as the most important benefit associations provide to an entire field, with committee-level people right behind them. A chasm of difference separates them from the other two segments. The ad hoc volunteers place greater importance on benefits that reflect the activities in which they are involved (writing, presentations, etc.). Their top-ranked activity in this category deals with producing trends data on the field. This is one of several activities that may be for the good of the order but has more immediate value for individuals that serve in this way (Exhibit 4.17).

EXHIBIT 4.17

How IMPORTANT were [would be] the following benefits to your field or profession in your decision to join?
(Rated on 1-5 scale with 5=very important. Mean rating shown. Asked about a particular association to both members and nonmembers. All are significantly different by volunteer activity.)

	Governance		Committee		Ad hoc		None	
	Mean	Rank	Mean	Rank	Mean	Rank	Mean	Rank
Promoting a greater appreciation of the role and value of the field among practitioners	3.96	1	3.95	2	3.53	6	3.68	4
Providing standards or guidelines that support quality	3.93	2	3.97	1	3.60	3	3.85	1
Maintaining a code of ethics for practice	3.91	3	3.86	5	3.42	7	3.74	2
Influencing legislation and regulations that affect the field	3.89	4	3.88	4	3.35	9	3.58	7
Promoting greater public awareness of contributions in the field	3.88	5	3.91	3	3.58	4	3.58	6
Supporting student education and entry into the field	3.72	6	3.78	6	3.55	5	3.52	8
Certifying those who meet critical competency standards	3.68	7	3.63	10	3.10	11	3.51	9
Gathering, analyzing and publishing data on trends in the field	3.68	8	3.78	7	3.68	1	3.73	3
Attracting competent people into the field	3.66	9	3.69	8	3.40	8	3.43	11
Conducting research on significant issues affecting the field	3.60	10	3.66	9	3.67	2	3.63	5
The association's role in defining critical competencies	3.55	11	3.59	11	3.18	10	3.43	10
Providing awards or recognition for excellence in the field	3.20	12	3.25	12	3.08	12	2.95	12

While respondents answered these questions in reference to a particular association, most associations provide some or all of these benefits to all in their industry or field. There are clear differences in priority (rank) at every volunteer level, even between those serving at the board and committee levels, particularly about maintaining a code of ethics and certification (both of which are more important to board-level volunteers). Ad hoc volunteers, who are more likely to be found among those in an academic environment (see Exhibit 7.5) clearly diverge in the priority they place on gathering, analyzing, and publishing data (one of the components of ad hoc volunteering). Those who don't volunteer at all also place more importance on gathering, analyzing, and publishing data than do either board- or committee-level volunteers.

Mean shows the average rating on a 1-5 scale with 5=very important. Rank is the order of priority. "Significant" differences in this and all tables refers to a finding of statistically significant differences based on the application of an appropriate statistical test.

As discussed earlier, people involved at the highest level may take on a more collective view of the association's activities, one that reflects their leadership responsibilities and thereby differs with the personal perspective of most other respondents. This concept may account for the differences in the way leaders at the governing level rank the importance of these activities as compared with other respondents.

Several important observations stem from this comparison. All of them are conjectural but worth raising for discussion:

1. The first has already been made. Leaders do have a different perspective, and it is one that indicates greater concern for the good of the order, which is both laudable and an expectation of leadership.

2. The second is that governance-level people who think they don't need empirical data on the way rank-and-file members evaluate the importance of programs, because as elected leaders they are in touch with the rank-and-file that elected them, might be well advised to look closely at the difference between their views and nearly everyone else's.

3. The third may be a small point, but the extreme difference between leaders and everyone else on the importance of "gathering, analyzing, and publishing data on trends in the field" is curious. Why is there such a difference? This is a strength of many trade associations, and many observers have noted that individual membership organizations could do a better job of this. Perhaps the rank-and-file in individual membership organizations agree.

Chapter Summary

1. Overall, former and never members see associations very favorably, with high positives and low negatives. People who have dropped membership in any association view associations in a less favorable light than never members.

2. Former members are apt to be more difficult to recruit back into membership because they place less value on timely information about the field, which is the strongest benefit of many associations.

3. One half of the current members who have at some point in the past dropped membership in an association did so for reasons having to do with that association's performance; the other half did so for reasons that had little to do with the association's performance. For former members (not current in any associations), 55 percent dropped for reasons that did not reflect on satisfaction with the association's performance.

4. Never members are less apt to be found in the private sector and more apt than current members to be among the nonprofits.

5. Former members are more likely to be employed by organizations that don't pay dues and never members are less likely to know whether their employers provide support, probably because they have not asked.

6. Advocacy, networking, and opportunities to gain leadership experience are benefits that become significantly more important as level of involvement increases.

7. Probability of being a "promoter" of the association increases with level of involvement. Members who do not become involved in their association are very similar to nonmembers in the way they rate the overall value of associations. In answering the "promoter" question—*Would you recommend the association to a colleague?*—they are far less apt to say yes than those who have been involved at any level. Because word-of-mouth from a colleague is the primary influence that motivates people to join, uninvolved people represent a drag on the potential recruiting power of the association.

8. Governance and committee volunteers place a much higher level of importance on benefits to the field such as advocacy to the public and the government than do those who accept ad hoc volunteer assignments. Selling the value of these benefits to ad hoc volunteers may provide the greatest opportunity to increase the "good of the order" index rating, thereby increasing member loyalty to the association.

9. The value of networking increases significantly with level of involvement, as does the importance of leadership opportunities. While all respondents say networking is important, those who actually do it through their association involvement come to value networking even more highly and may, as a consequence, develop a greater appreciation for the value of leadership experience.

10. Leaders who are involved at the governing level give different importance ratings to both personal and good-of-the-order benefits than
do the majority of members who are not involved. An example of this
includes the higher importance rating they give to "representing the
field within the industry or discipline," which effectively means dealing
with the struggles among various disciplines that they as leaders are
responsible for addressing. It may be important for them to understand
the extent to which their responsibilities affect their perspective, which
means that they may not, as some may assume, be in sync with the
members they represent.

CHAPTER 5

Generations and Career Level

Two methods of analyzing differences in populations based on needs are considered. The first is based on the idea that each generation has a unique profile with respect to their view of the world, which translates into criteria that would affect their decisions to join an association. The second is based on the more traditional idea of career development stages that dictate a predictable set of needs as age groups move through them. The probability of young people joining associations in the future as they have in the past is explored. A comparison between entry- and mid-level ratings of association benefits with the ratings given by senior-level people who are more frequently found among those who govern associations is provided to reveal the specific issues associations may need to address to attract younger, entry-, and mid-level members more effectively.

O NE OF THE GREATEST fears expressed by association leaders in recent years has been the prospect of declining membership owing to younger generations that no longer find value in the association experience. Much of this concern is fueled by the popularity of categorization schemes that assign unique psychographic characteristics to generational age groupings, marking them with identity tags that they carry with them for life. Since every generation is different, every future generation will require deciphering and tagging. This approach is at odds with a more traditional classification system that assumes people acquire distinct needs as they move through age-related phases of development. The generational model focuses on permanent characteristics that influence preferences. The career model looks more directly at needs that change across time in a fairly predictable manner. The concept of generational stereotyping has captured a great deal of attention in recent years, either because of its novelty or the direness of its implications. The chances that associations may be facing a lost generation or the end of membership as it has been known for eons is the marketing equivalent of a sky that is falling, and fear has a way of capturing one's attention.

It is a fact that people under 30 are not joining associations at the same rate that people older than 30 are, which means that the under-30 age group is significantly underrepresented in many associations. Is this because unique differences exist in the generational characteristics of young people, or has the entry-level age group always been slow to join associations?

At least three significantly different strategy-making scenarios lie in waiting for a reliable answer to this question. The first scenario comes into play if the current cohort of young people is indeed different in ways that leave them permanently less inclined to join associations. In the worst version of this scenario, they may already see associations as lumbering old anachronisms, out of touch with their needs and riding into yesterday like an Oldsmobile. On the brighter side of this scenario, some optimists buy into the generational differences model and yet believe it is not too late to mitigate this dire fate. But it will require considerable research into the unique needs of this generation, followed by the prospect of substantial investments to retool the product and service line accordingly.

The second scenario is based on the career stages model, and it assumes that the younger generation will grow into membership as they enter the stages that associations have traditionally focused on and served fairly well. If this seems a bit too complacent—effectively saying "stay cool and let them come to us"—a more assertive strategy option can be added. It would have associations acknowledge the probability of an age bias in the programs that they offer and work harder to serve the entry-level needs that the younger age group has always had. This too requires research, but it's much easier to understand needs that have not been served adequately than it is to decipher a one-of-a-kind generation.

The third scenario is simply an enhanced version of the second. It also uses the career model but goes on to assume that the world is changing in ways that are restructuring service-delivery methods and expectations for everyone. Digital information and electronic communication technologies offer alternative ways of affiliating with others and gaining access to exploding amounts and sources of information. It may well be that the generation just entering membership eligibility is the first to have fully internalized these changes before encountering the decision to join, but that's an ephemeral moment in time, not an enduring "Gen Y" or "Millennial" attribute. The technology paradigm is shifting for everyone, and there is now evidence to show that the older age groups are no longer as techno-naive as the commonly held stereotypes imply. Findings from this survey and other relevant sources seem to favor this scenario.

One of the more thorough studies of generational differences as they are apt to affect the decision to join an association was commissioned by SmithBucklin and conducted by Arthur C. Brooks, PhD in 2006.[1] Brooks analyzed as a part of this study the "largest and most comprehensive datasets available on civic life in the United States" and concluded the following:

> *Generation X and Y workers*[2] *show great promise to join associations as they move into their peak earning years. Correcting for race, gender, education, political views, religious beliefs, marital status, and family size, the data reveal that Generation X and Y workers are not inherently less likely than Baby Boomers to join associations. On the contrary, given rising incomes and improving job opportunities, young workers show every indication of joining associations at even higher rates than the Baby Boomers, more than making up for their slightly smaller numbers. The bottom line is that fear over the effects of Generation X and Y on association membership is not warranted.*

The study not only negates the first scenario's assumption that inherent differences would incline younger generations to pass on association memberships, it clearly documents the second scenario's premise that entry-level age groups are simply slow to join. Brooks cites the Social Capital and Community Benchmark Survey (SCCBS) undertaken in the year 2000 by a researchers' collaboration with the Roper Center for Public Opinion Research and the Saguaro Seminar at Harvard University's Kennedy School of Government. At that time Generations X and Y had significantly lower association membership rates than the Baby Boomers, which could be construed to support the notion that they are inherently different. He points out, however, that in the year 2000, the Generation X respondents were between 25 and 35 years of age. Four years later at Syracuse University, Brooks conducted a similar study that confirmed most of the SCCBS findings except for one notable exception. The four-year time lapse moved most of the Generation X population past the age of 30, and with that as the only discernable difference, they surged ahead of the Baby Boomers in terms of their association membership. From this and our study we agree wholeheartedly with Brooks' conclusion that needs

---

[1] *Generations and the Future of Association Participation*, Arthur C. Brooks, PhD, published by The William E. Smith Institute for Association Research; Copyright © 2006 SmithBucklin Corporation.

[2] Generations X and Y include those born after 1965 and 1975 respectively.

associated with stages of career development are the drivers, not fixed generational attributes.

The ASAE & The Center study addressed the question of age and career level, as expected, found a strong correlation between the two. The younger the respondent, the more likely they were to be at the entry level.

EXHIBIT 5.1

Correlation Between Age and Career Level

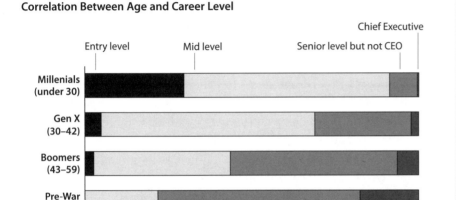

Because career level was not asked of a large proportion of respondents (those in academia, the self employed in private industry, the unemployed, and retired respondents) we focus on age—a question asked of all respondents and answered by more than 90 percent of them in this chapter.

EXHIBIT 5.2

Respondent Age

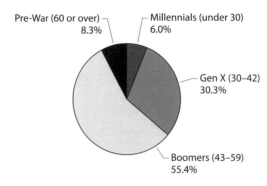

EXHIBIT 5.3

Respondent Career Level

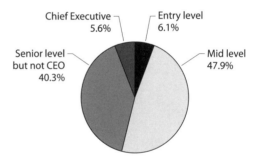

The survey questions regarding the overarching value of associations support the notion of a surge in the entry-level age groups' interest in associations at about the time they've clarified their career paths and are coming to understand what that requires. Three of the "overarching value" questions reflect on this emerging awareness (Exhibit 5.4).

When asked about their perception of the overall value that associations deliver, the responses to the first question shows an age-sensitive progression that moves from a modest level of appreciation on the younger side of the spectrum to much more favorable sentiments as the age of the respondent population matures. Appreciation of associations increases with age.

EXHIBIT 5.4

Overarching Value Questions by Age
(All are significantly different.)

	Millennials (under 30)	Gen X (30–42)	Boomers (43–59)	Pre-War (60 or over)
What is your overall attitude toward associations? *(5-point scale, 5='very favorable')*				
Mean	4.02	4.00	4.04	4.09
(% 'very favorable')	30.1%	31.5%	36.7%	42.9%
Do you believe associations are capable of addressing the practical needs of individual members? *(5-point scale, 5='definitely yes')*				
Mean	3.75	3.78	3.92	4.03
(% 'definitely yes')	18.5%	21.5%	29.7%	36.2%
Would you say that there are too many associations in your professional area of interest, too few, or is the number about right? *(No answer excluded.)*				
Too many	9.5%	13.6%	15.1%	18.6%
Too few	14.8%	12.2%	9.0%	4.8%
About right	75.8%	74.2%	75.9%	76.6%
Do you think there will be a greater or lesser need for associations five years from now? *(No answer excluded.)*				
Greater	41.9%	38.2%	37.0%	37.9%
Lesser	7.0%	7.0%	10.1%	11.8%
About the same	51.2%	54.7%	52.9%	50.3%

Both attitude toward associations and the belief that they are capable of addressing the needs of individuals increase with age. The perception that there are "too many" associations in respondent's professional area of interest also increases with age. An important ray of good news is found in the increasing perception of a "greater" need for associations in the future as age declines, particularly among millennials who are most likely to be found in the never member category now.

"Significant" differences in this and all tables refers to a finding of statistically significant differences based on the application of an appropriate statistical test.

When asked the more demanding question about the capability of associations in addressing the practical needs of individuals, all four age groups become more reserved in their judgment. Subtracting the percentage of 'definitely yes' responses from the percentage of 'very favorable' would show another age-sensitive progression in the level of decline from the general question to the more specific one. In comparison, the two youngest age groups dropped more precipitously than the others. It could be that they are more inclined to disagree with the statement or that they simply don't have as much information or experience with associations as the respondents in the two older groups.

In the third question "too many" generally implies that there are more associations than the respondents feel they need, while "too few" indicates that the respondents have needs that they do not believe are being addressed by the associations that they are aware of, so there aren't enough. Again, the responses are age sensitive on an incline that suggests that the younger people may be more apt to think the association options available to them do not adequately address their needs.

When asked to look five years into the future and anticipate the need for associations at that time, the youngest generation surges forward from its lagging estimation of value from associations to take the lead position by a significant margin. What could possibly account for this? The idea of five years into the future may carry different connotations for each age group. For the oldest, the relevance of an association probably declines with the prospects of retirement. So the age group that consistently gives associations the highest estimations of value drops into parity with the next two age groups. Respondents in their mid 40s and 50s may be at a point where they can see the peak of their careers or possibly sense that they are there, which may have a moderating effect on their five-year appraisal of value of associations to them. That the third age group is equivalent to the older two may indicate that "the future" is a concept that begins to homogenize and flatten out for everyone once a certain age is achieved.

The youngest age group presents a very different profile. For them to see a significantly greater need for associations when they look five years into the future indicates a surge in awareness that corresponds to the surge in memberships found in the Brooks study once young professionals moved from their mid-20s into their 30s. In that analysis, a retrospective metric based on membership was used to predict with confidence that an age-related surge occurs in the appeal of associations as people move toward completion of their entry-level career phase. In this study, a prospective metric regarding the perception of future needs indicates a similar phenomenon. All other age groups settle into a common view of the future on this point except for the youngest. It's as if adrenalin kicks in with the eye-opening realization that the future poses challenges that may warrant a little help from some friends and that a vehicle for this is in place through joining an association.

Association Functions

Discovering that associations provide the possibility of much-needed help does not mean that the youngest age group has the same needs as those in the other career stages. The survey question dealing with predisposition toward associations in general and the two questions regarding the perception of value delivered by a specific association in their field sheds light on respondent needs and the extent to which they think associations address them.

In the question regarding respondents' estimation of associations in general, it is assumed that the older groups are reflecting what they believe associations do best based on their experience with them, while the youngest group, whose association experience is more limited, reflects an appraisal that is more likely to be influenced by their expectations. The percentage data in Exhibit 5.5 show the frequency with which respondents chose a particular function when given a list of nine and asked to select the three that they believed were "the most important functions" of an association.

In comparing the top four selections made by the youngest group with others, we see some divergent views. All but the oldest agree on the primary importance of providing training/professional development to members, a personal benefit to individuals. The youngest group maintains an emphasis on personal benefits in their second choice by selecting networking, while the older groups opt for providing technical information to members, the third-ranked function for millennials. The groups diverge on the fourth function, with the youngest group opting for the common good function of representing the field to the public. It may be that the younger

generation would like the pride they have for their field to be more visible in the public's awareness. The older group may have come to realize that the resources available to most associations simply don't allow for having great impact on public awareness. Their top choices probably give a more

EXHIBIT 5.5

What do you think are the most important functions of an association?
(Respondents selected up to 3 choices. Significant differences in bold.)

	Millennials (under 30)		Gen X (30–42)		Boomers (43–59)		Pre-War (60 or over)	
	%	Rank	%	Rank	%	Rank	%	Rank
Providing training/ professional development to members	50.0%	1	44.7%	1	46.6%	1	45.3%	2
Connecting practitioners within the field to each other/networking	41.0%	2	37.7%	3	35.3%	4	34.1%	4
Providing technical information to members	38.7%	3	40.6%	2	44.9%	2	49.5%	1
Representing the field to the public	34.3%	4	30.4%	6	24.7%	7	28.1%	6
Providing timely information about the field to members	31.0%	5	35.7%	4	37.1%	3	42.8%	3
Creating and disseminating standards of practice	26.1%	6	30.9%	5	32.5%	5	27.0%	7
Representing the field to the government	24.8%	7	28.2%	7	28.0%	6	30.0%	5
Providing certification opportunities	21.9%	8	19.1%	9	19.8%	9	16.2%	9
Representing the field within the industry or discipline	21.9%	9	21.2%	8	20.8%	8	16.6%	8

Professional development and networking are more likely to be perceived by the youngest respondents as the primary functions of an association. Since this group is also most likely to be among the never members appealing to these already held beliefs would likely hold some promise in recruiting them. Representing the field to the public is function where we see a lot of divergence between the youngest group and all others.

Percent % shows the frequency the item was checked by each type of respondent. Rank is the order of priority. "Significant" differences in this and all tables refers to a finding of statistically significant differences based on the application of an appropriate statistical test.

accurate reflection of what associations do best. At any rate, in trying to understand how the expectations of the youngest age groups differ from the rest, placing greater importance on public awareness of their field constitutes one such difference.

Personal Benefits

The distinction between direct personal benefits to the individual and serving the common good by providing benefits to an entire field was less apparent in the question regarding associations in general (Exhibit 5.5). When the frame of reference shifted to a specific association, the activities that respondents were given to evaluate were more detailed, the response options more explicit, and separate questions were used to distinguish personal benefits from benefits to the field. The more explicit response options had the respondents evaluate the activities twice: once according to the importance of the activity and then according to their perception of a particular association's performance in delivering on that expectation. Both appraisals used similar five-point scales, from which a performance gap was calculated by subtracting the mean score for performance from the mean score for importance. A negative gap measure indicates that performance fails to meet the expectations driven by the importance. The gap analysis is shown in this chapter and no other because, for the most part, few negative gaps were found by the segments under study. This was not the case by age, where we see significant gaps when those who are members of a particular association rated the importance of several of the personal and good-of-the-order benefits and then rated their association's performance on that measure. Note that all respondents rated importance, but only members of a particular association rated satisfaction. Thus, the gap is only calculated for members.

From the list of eight activities that provide direct personal benefit, five are significant in showing how the expressed needs of the youngest age group differs from the rest, as seen in Exhibit 5.6.

Activities in the table are in order of their importance to the youngest age group. Observations on the age differences include the following:

- *Access to the most up to date information available in your field:* This is the most important personal benefit to respondents in all age groups. While a negative gap is commonly seen in the most important activity, what differentiates this activity for the youngest group is the fact that the performance gap they report is twice what it is for the other age groups.

- *Professional development or educational program offerings:* The slope of the importance measure from high to low tracks by age, with the youngest group reporting the highest importance score. While this distinguishes them from the others, the more pronounced difference is in their negative gap. Traditionally, the cost of delivering professional development, particularly with respect to travel expenses, has biased this activity toward the older groups that have lower levels of need. Internet delivery of this activity may provide one of the best opportunities for associations to recruit and serve the youngest age group if the issue is delivery. If the issue is content, something greater is needed. This study is silent on this question. Associations need to determine which is more applicable.

- *Access to career information and employment opportunities:* Again, the slope of the importance measure tracks by age, which is to be expected given the nature of the activity. This is the third most important activity for the youngest age group, and they are alone in placing it that high in the rank order of all eight activities. They are the only age group to give it a negative performance gap. Of the four program activities that distinguish their needs, this may provide the least expensive one for the association to provide more effectively and for the member to access most readily.

- *Opportunities for you to network with other professionals in your field:* The same observations as made for career information and opportunities listed above apply here. A focus on entry- to mid-level career needs should be the emphasis of these activities.

Exhibit 5.6 and the observations made from it provide the clearest opportunities for associations to strengthen the appeal of the programs that they offer the youngest generation that is, for most associations, an underrepresented segment.

EXHIBIT 5.6

How IMPORTANT* were [would be*] the following personal benefits in your decision to join?

(Rated on 1-5 scale with 5=very important. Mean rating shown. Asked about a particular association to both members and nonmembers. Significant differences in bold.)

After rating importance, members were asked to rate their SATISFACTION with their association's delivery of that benefit to them. The mean GAP (satisfaction minus importance) is shown.

	Millennials (under 30)		Gen X (30–42)		Boomers (43–59)		Pre-War (60 or over)	
	Mean	Rank	Mean	Rank	Mean	Rank	Mean	Rank
Access to the most up to date information available in your field	**4.27**	**1**	**4.19**	**1**	**4.22**	**1**	**4.24**	**1**
Gap	-0.21		-0.11		-0.08		-0.10	
Professional development or educational program offerings	**4.13**	**2**	**3.93**	**2**	**3.91**	**2**	**3.71**	**2**
Gap	-0.23		-0.14		-0.03		0.07	
Access to career information and employment opportunities	**4.03**	**3**	**3.61**	**4**	**3.30**	**4**	**2.76**	**7**
Gap	-0.20		0.07		0.26		0.49	
Opportunities for you to network with other professionals in your field	**3.93**	**4**	**3.74**	**3**	**3.69**	**3**	**3.65**	**3**
Gap	-0.15		0.04		0.11		0.15	
Opportunities to gain leadership experience	**3.37**	**5**	**3.14**	**6**	**3.01**	**6**	**2.76**	**6**
Gap	0.08		0.24		0.46		0.60	
Access to products, services, and suppliers (e.g., insurance, publications, etc.)	3.36	6	3.25	5	3.20	5	3.07	4
Gap	0.48		0.50		0.55		0.58	
Member discounts or group purchasing activities	3.25	7	2.99	7	2.78	8	2.50	8
Gap	0.31		0.52		0.71		0.78	
A reference directory of members/practitioners	3.10	8	2.93	8	2.90	7	2.91	5
Gap	0.64		0.68		0.70		0.65	

Gap is the average difference between the mean importance rating and member rating of satisfaction with a particular association's performance. In most of this survey the gaps were positive (see Exhibit B.9 in Appendix B). A negative gap means that member satisfaction ratings were lower than member importance ratings. This is the only chapter in which the gap was relevant to the segment analysis. This table clearly shows some vulnerability for associations among the youngest members, particularly in the areas of professional development, career and employment information, and networking. "Access to the most up to date information" is also a high negative gap item (increasing in severity for the youngest members), although a negative gap is commonly found in gap analysis on the most important benefit. Note that, unlike the importance measure which was asked of all respondents, the gap is only based on member ratings because only members rated the performance of an association to which they belonged.

Mean shows the average rating on a 1-5 scale with 5=very important. Rank is the order of priority. "Significant" differences in this and all tables refers to a finding of statistically significant differences based on the application of an appropriate statistical test.

Benefits to Field

In the generalized view taken of all associations, the youngest age group distinguishes itself by placing public awareness as the fourth most frequently selected "important" association function (see Exhibit 5.5). And, as shown in Exhibit 5.7, they demonstrate consistency by rating public awareness the third most important good-of-the-order benefit delivered by a particular association that serves their field. While all four age groups are fairly even in the importance that they assign to public awareness, the youngest differentiate themselves again with respect to the negative performance gap they give it.

More noteworthy, however, is their rating of support for student education and entry into the field. Being so close in their memory of this phase of life it comes as no surprise that they rate it higher and see the association's performance in a negative light. More significant is the fact that from among the 12 activities listed in this question, the youngest ranked it number one in importance, while their peers in the next age group ranked it 7th, followed by 8th for the next group and 9th for the oldest. How quickly this fades in importance! Nevertheless, facilitating programs where the youngest are called upon to mentor the transition of students into the field is a role many associations assume should go to people in older, more experienced age groups. Maybe it is from the standpoint of students. But from the standpoint of the youngest age group, this is an activity that they care deeply about and one where they have transition experiences—lessons learned—that are probably worth sharing. It also may address their need for more leadership opportunities.

EXHIBIT 5.7

How IMPORTANT* were [would be*] the following benefits to your field or profession in your decision to join?

(Rated on 1-5 scale with 5=very important. Mean rating shown. Asked about a particular association to both members and nonmembers. Significant differences in bold.)

After rating importance, members were asked to rate their SATISFACTION with their association's delivery of that benefit to them. The mean GAP (satisfaction minus importance) is shown.

	Millennials (under 30)		Gen X (30–42)		Boomers (43–59)		Pre-War (60 or over)	
	Mean	Rank	Mean	Rank	Mean	Rank	Mean	Rank
Supporting student education and entry into the field	**3.94**	**1**	**3.63**	**7**	**3.53**	**8**	**3.44**	**9**
Gap	-0.12	1	0.11	7	0.20	8	0.27	9
Providing standards or guidelines that support quality	**3.90**	**2**	**3.81**	**1**	**3.87**	**1**	**3.83**	**1**
Gap	-0.03	2	0.04	1	0.05	1	0.07	1
Promoting greater public awareness of contributions in the field	**3.87**	**3**	**3.70**	**4**	**3.64**	**7**	**3.59**	**6**
Gap	-0.28	3	-0.14	4	-0.09	7	-0.04	6
Promoting a greater appreciation of the role and value of the field among practitioners	**3.84**	**4**	**3.70**	**5**	**3.70**	**4**	**3.60**	**5**
Gap	-0.10	4	-0.02	5	0.01	4	0.14	5
Maintaining a code of ethics for practice	3.80	5	3.69	6	3.76	3	3.76	2
Gap	0.14	5	0.20	6	0.17	3	0.16	2
Gathering, analyzing, and publishing data on trends in the field	3.79	6	3.75	2	3.79	2	3.70	3
Gap	0.16	6	0.19	2	0.20	2	0.26	3
Conducting research on significant issues affecting the field	3.79	7	3.71	3	3.69	5	3.64	4
Gap	0.09	7	0.13	3	0.18	5	0.19	4
Attracting competent people into the field	3.73	8	3.55	9	3.51	10	3.45	8
Gap	-0.07	8	0.07	9	0.09	10	0.13	8
Influencing legislation and regulations that affect the field	3.72	9	3.60	8	3.67	6	3.59	7
Gap	-0.04	9	-0.04	8	0.03	6	0.11	7
Certifying those who meet critical competency standards	3.71	10	3.54	10	3.51	9	3.40	11
Gap	0.05	10	0.13	10	0.20	9	0.27	11
The association's role in defining critical competencies	3.53	11	3.42	11	3.45	11	3.42	10
Gap	0.17	11	0.27	11	0.27	11	0.28	10
Providing awards or recognition for excellence in the field	3.34	12	3.12	12	3.02	12	2.99	12
Gap	0.55	12	0.66	12	0.74	12	0.73	12

Gap is the average difference between the mean importance rating and member rating of satisfaction with a particular association's performance. In most of this survey the gap was positive (see Exhibit B.10 in Appendix B). A negative gap means that member satisfaction ratings were lower than member importance ratings. This is the only chapter in which the gap was relevant to the segment analysis. There is clear vulnerability for associations among the youngest members, particularly in the area of "promoting greater public awareness of the field." Note that, unlike the importance measure which was asked of all respondents, the gap is only based on member ratings because only members rated the performance of their association on the measure.

Mean shows the average rating on a 1-5 scale with 5=very important. Rank is the order of priority. "Significant" differences in this and all tables refers to a finding of statistically significant differences based on the application of an appropriate statistical test.

Preferred Means of Getting Information

The assumption that the youngest age group is much more comfortable with electronic technologies is called into question by a survey finding on how respondents "prefer to receive information about your profession or field" (Exhibit 5.8). A rank ordering of various communication options shows little difference in the way the youngest compare with a much older group. The stronger preference that the older group expresses for electronic newsletters is particularly significant and should offer comfort to the CFOs who are pushing to get out from under the cost of print publications.

EXHIBIT 5.8

How do you prefer to receive information about your profession or field?
(Respondents selected up to 3 choices. Significant differences in bold.)

	Millennials (under 30)		Gen X (30–42)		Boomers (43–59)		Pre-War (60 or over)	
	%	Rank	%	Rank	%	Rank	%	Rank
In magazines or journals serving your field	64.1%	1	64.9%	1	64.9%	1	67.4%	1
At Conferences or meetings	49.7%	2	51.0%	3	55.3%	2	57.0%	2
In E-newsletters	46.5%	3	52.0%	2	54.3%	3	52.5%	3
Through an association Web site	45.3%	4	46.9%	4	48.8%	4	42.8%	4
By searching on the Internet	20.5%	5	18.6%	5	16.2%	5	15.3%	5
Through your network of peers (word of mouth)	15.4%	6	12.3%	6	11.7%	7	13.9%	6
Through communities of practice (e.g. special interest groups, user groups, etc.)	10.0%	7	10.9%	7	12.5%	6	13.3%	7
In print sources other than magazines or newspapers	6.5%	8	6.5%	8	6.1%	8	7.9%	8
In general interest magazines	5.2%	9	4.6%	9	3.5%	9	3.6%	9
In newspapers (print)	4.5%	10	3.4%	10	2.9%	10	3.0%	10
Through blogs or podcasts	3.3%	12	2.5%	11	1.9%	11	1.0%	11
Through traditional broadcast media (television or radio)	4.0%	11	2.0%	12	1.4%	12	1.0%	12

Although there are significant differences in the frequency of selecting the top three preferences for receiving information, they are only marginally different. Preferences are clear: magazines and journals, conferences and meetings and e-newsletters top the source preferences for all age groups.

Percent % shows the frequency the item was checked by each type of respondent. Rank is the order of priority. "Significant" differences in this and all tables refers to a finding of statistically significant differences based on the application of an appropriate statistical test.

Chapter Summary

1. The perception of the value of associations increases with age in all but one of the overarching value questions. Asked about the need for associations five years from now, the youngest age group gives an importance rating that surges ahead of all other age groups. This corresponds with other research indicating that this awakening regarding the value of associations occurs in the late 20s to early 30s. The strategic issue for associations is whether they can continue to wait for the surge to take place or, given the proliferation of competing sources of information and networking opportunities, whether they need to improve their benefits in ways that attract the younger much sooner.

2. The analysis by age is the only demographic characteristic in this study in which noteworthy negative gaps are found in the ratings members give for both personal and good-of-the-order benefits between the importance of the benefit and satisfaction with their organization's performance.

3. The importance and satisfaction ratings that these age-based segments give for personal benefits shows much greater variance among the age groups than the benefits to the field. Respondents indicate that improving the appeal of associations and thereby recruiting them more effectively at a younger age will require strengthening four of the eight personal benefits:

   - *Access to the most up to date information available in your field*
   - *Professional development or educational program offerings*
   - *Access to career information and employment opportunities*
   - *Opportunities for you to network with other professionals in your field*

4. Of the 12 benefits to the field, four stood out as differentiating the age-based segments with negative gaps decreasing with age for two of them:

   - *Supporting student education and entry into the field*
   - *Promoting greater public awareness of contributions in the field*

5. The assumption that the younger age group is more comfortable with emerging technologies is not supported.

CHAPTER 6

Gender

How do males and females differ, in this case with respect to their perceptions of the value they find in associations? On the surface, the differences are subtle. When the segmentation is augmented to recognize gender-dominant work settings, a much stronger set of differences emerge. Much conjecture flows and may continue to flow from these limited but clearly established facts. Women in female-dominant settings give higher importance ratings on nearly all benefits and place greater emphasis on collective actions for the common good. Despite this apparent adamancy, their age demographics show lower levels of entry-level people. Males in female-dominant settings show similar levels of conviction, giving higher value ratings than males in integrated settings. Males in male-dominant settings are the most complacent of all in terms of their benefit value ratings.

EXHIBIT 6.1

What is your gender?

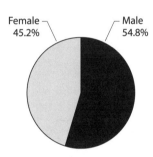

Female 45.2%   Male 54.8%

A T FIRST GLANCE, GENDER appears to have little influence on an individual's decision to join a professional association. The three most telling indicators of this come from the questions dealing with the challenges professionals see in their environment, the association activities that deliver direct personal value, and the activities that deliver value more broadly to the entire field or discipline.

Males and females place the challenges in much the same order of importance (Exhibit 6.2). And only 5 of the 16 challenges that face their professional community are significantly different in frequency. Three of these are noteworthy because the differences in frequency also result in large differences in rank.

- Men rank "an expanding body of knowledge" and "increasing competition" higher than women.
- Women rank "lack of public awareness in your field" higher than men.
- Men rank "increasing competition" higher than women.

In responses to the question regarding direct personal benefits provided by a particular association, males and females place all eight program activities in the same order of importance; although the females assign a higher level of importance to all of them, the order of priority remains the same as for males (Exhibit 6.3).

In the question regarding good-of-the-order benefits (Exhibit 6.4), females once again give significantly higher importance ratings to all 12 of these activities, but the pattern of rank ordering is also different. Significant gender differences include the following:

- Men rank "gathering, analyzing, and publishing data on trends in the field" and "conducting research on significant issues affecting the field" higher than women.
- Women rank "maintaining a code of ethics for practice," "promoting a greater appreciation of the role and value of the field among practitioners," and "influencing legislation and regulations that affect the field" higher than men.

EXHIBIT 6.2

Select the top three challenges that face your professional community.
(Respondents selected up to 3 choices. Significant differences in bold.)

	Male		Female	
	%	Rank	%	Rank
Inadequate recognition of the value delivered by the profession or discipline to the larger society	31.8%	1	36.9%	1
Keeping up with new information in the field	31.3%	2	33.4%	2
Inadequate sources of funding or revenue	24.9%	3	21.5%	5
Keeping pace with technology	23.1%	4	23.9%	4
An expanding body of knowledge	**22.4%**	**5**	**17.3%**	**8**
Lack of public awareness of your field	**21.8%**	**6**	**26.3%**	**3**
Increasing competition (domestic or international)	**17.6%**	**7**	**11.4%**	**11**
Cost containment pressures	16.7%	8	16.5%	9
Achieving high-quality outcomes	16.2%	9	13.2%	10
Challenging regulatory environment (needed relief from regulations)	16.2%	10	18.4%	7
Inadequate supply of capable professionals	16.1%	11	19.6%	6
Rapidly changing, difficult to predict market conditions or trends	13.4%	12	10.5%	13
Liability exposure, risk management	12.1%	13	10.9%	12
Inadequate supply of support personnel	7.7%	14	9.3%	14
Undesirable pending legislation	7.0%	15	7.1%	16
Technology replacing practitioners	**4.2%**	**16**	**8.1%**	**15**

Five of the sixteen challenges resulted in significant differences in frequency and of them, three also resulted in large differences in rank.

Percent % shows the frequency the item was checked by each type of respondent. Rank is the order of priority. "Significant" differences in this and all tables refers to a finding of statistically significant differences based on the application of an appropriate statistical test.

EXHIBIT 6.3

How IMPORTANT were [would be] the following personal benefits in your decision to join?
(Rated on 1-5 scale with 5=very important. Mean rating shown. Asked about a particular association to both members and nonmembers. All ratings are significantly different.)

	Male		Female	
	Mean	Rank	Mean	Rank
Access to the most up to date information available in your field	4.11	1	4.35	1
Professional development or educational program offerings	3.67	2	4.18	2
Opportunities for you to network with other professionals in your field	3.63	3	3.84	3
Access to career information and employment opportunities	3.20	4	3.62	4
Access to products, services, and suppliers (e.g. insurance, publications, etc.)	3.11	5	3.34	5
Opportunities to gain leadership experience	2.91	6	3.22	6
A reference directory of members/practitioners	2.81	7	3.08	7
Member discounts or group purchasing activities	2.69	8	3.04	8

While respondents answered these questions in reference to a particular association, most associations offer some or all of the personal benefits listed here. All respondents answered questions about the importance of these personal benefits regardless of member status. Women give higher ratings for all personal benefits, but the rank order is the same for both genders.

Mean shows the average rating on a 1-5 scale with 5=very important. Rank is the order of priority. "Significant" differences in this and all tables refers to a finding of statistically significant differences based on the application of an appropriate statistical test.

Two generalizations may account for these observations. By placing greater emphasis on government affairs and the need to promote greater appreciation for the field among both the public and the variety of practitioners who work together, women appear to put greater emphasis on the need to take actions that will change their environment. Men, on the other hand, seem to emphasize the need for information regarding the environment they find themselves in. One implies the need for collective

action and the other a need to influence the immediate environment. At this point, these observations provide fairly scant information for theory building, but a theme is introduced that takes on further momentum when other perspectives are introduced.

The Influence of Gender-Dominant Work Settings

The 18 associations that participated in this study have reliable data on the gender balance of both their associations and the fields they represent, which was also validated by the ratio of male-to-female respondents in this study. This information allowed for the identification of respondents who were members or potential members of associations predominantly composed of a single gender and, by extension and by confirmation from secondary data, who work in fields where the preponderant number of practitioners are one gender or the other. Associations with 75 percent or more respondents of a single gender were considered male or female dominant for this analysis.

This allowed for comparisons between respondents in "integrated" associations and fields and respondents in female- or male-dominant associations and fields. From this perspective, gender becomes a far more significant factor.

Women by Gender Mix

Without exception, females who were in female-dominant settings indicate that they received significantly greater value from their association experience than females in other settings, particularly when compared to females in male-dominant settings (Exhibit 6.6). The survey included questions in

EXHIBIT 6.4

How IMPORTANT were [would be] the following benefits to your field or profession in your decision to join?

(Rated on 1-5 scale with 5=very important. Mean rating shown. Asked about a particular association to both members and nonmembers. All ratings are significantly different.)

	Male		Female	
	Mean	Rank	Mean	Rank
Providing standards or guidelines that support quality	3.68	1	4.04	1
Gathering, analyzing and publishing data on trends in the field	3.68	2	3.87	5
Conducting research on significant issues affecting the field	3.60	3	3.81	7
Maintaining a code of ethics for practice	3.56	4	3.97	2
Promoting greater public awareness of contributions in the field	3.52	5	3.86	6
Promoting a greater appreciation of the role and value of the field among practitioners	3.51	6	3.93	3
Supporting student education and entry into the field	3.44	7	3.75	9
Influencing legislation and regulations that affect the field	3.42	8	3.91	4
Attracting competent people into the field	3.37	9	3.72	10
Certifying those who meet critical competency standards	3.28	10	3.81	8
The association's role in defining critical competencies	3.27	11	3.65	11
Providing awards or recognition for excellence in the field	2.95	12	3.22	12

While respondents answered these questions in reference to a particular association, most associations provide some or all of these benefits to all in their industry or field. All respondents answered questions about the importance of these benefits regardless of member status. As found with their ratings of personal benefits, covered in Exhibit 6.3, women generally give higher ratings on good-of-the-order benefits for every item than do men. They also prioritize these items differently with "maintaining a code of ethics for practice," "promoting a greater appreciation of the role and value of the field among practitioners" and "influencing legislation and regulations that affect the field" given a higher priority among women than among men.

Mean shows the average rating on a 1-5 scale with 5=very important. Rank is the order of priority. "Significant" differences in this and all tables refers to a finding of statistically significant differences based on the application of an appropriate statistical test.

EXHIBIT 6.5

Distribution of Women by Gender Dominance in Field

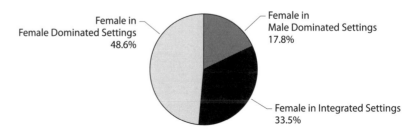

Female in Female Dominated Settings 48.6%

Female in Male Dominated Settings 17.8%

Female in Integrated Settings 33.5%

all three spheres that asked for overall perceptions of value. In every one of them, women in female-dominant settings indicated that they were more positive about their association experience than females in other settings and females in male-dominant settings were less positive.

Responses to these questions build a strong case for the assertion that females in female-dominant associations and fields think that they receive

EXHIBIT 6.6

Overarching Value Questions—Women by Gender Mix
(All are significantly different.)

	Women		
	In Integrated Settings	In Female-Dominant Settings	In Male-Dominant Settings
What is your overall attitude toward associations? *(5-point scale, 5='very favorable')*			
Mean	4.10	4.01	4.01
(% 'very favorable')	37.9%	40.4%	32.4%
Do you believe associations are capable of addressing the practical needs of individual members? *(5-point scale, 5= 'definitely yes')*			
Mean	3.94	3.95	3.72
(% 'definitely yes')	28.7%	34.3%	20.8%
Would you say that there are too many associations in your professional area of interest, too few, or is the number about right?			
Too many	13.3%	7.3%	16.7%
Too few	8.9%	16.5%	10.6%
About right	77.8%	76.2%	72.8%
Do you think there will be a greater or lesser need for associations five years from now?			
Greater	37.3%	48.2%	34.5%
Lesser	9.3%	6.3%	9.3%
About the same	53.4%	45.5%	56.1%

EXHIBIT 6.6 (continued)

	Women		
	In Integrated Settings	In Female-Dominant Settings	In Male-Dominant Settings
Have you ever dropped membership in any association?			
% Yes	56.4%	46.5%	50.7%
How likely is it that you would recommend membership in *[a particular association]* to a friend or colleague? *(10-point scale summarized. See* The Ultimate Question *by Fred Reichheld.)*			
Promoter (rating 9 or 10)	44.0%	55.9%	35.9%
Passive (rating 7 or 8)	31.2%	20.7%	32.9%
Detractor (rating 6 or lower)	24.7%	23.5%	31.2%

This table breaks female respondents into three groups: those in "integrated" settings (where men and women are both present), women in female-dominant settings (where women make up 75 percent or more of the field , and women in male-dominant settings (women make up 25 percent or less of the field). These data clearly suggest that women in female dominant fields are more positive about their association experience.

"Significant" differences in this and all tables refers to a finding of statistically significant differences based on the application of an appropriate statistical test.

greater value from their association than do females in other settings. If women in female-dominant settings are higher on their association experience, with many more willing to tell their colleagues to join, then one might reasonably expect such associations to have an edge in attracting younger members. But this is not the case. When gender balance is analyzed by the respondents' age groupings, the positive information coming from female-dominant associations raises some concern (Exhibit 6.7). Respondents in female-dominant fields are concentrated in the two older generations, while female membership in male-dominant fields is much more likely in the two younger age groups. Why isn't the higher perception of value having more influence on the identification of younger women in associations serving female-dominant fields? (Remember that co-sponsor organizations provided names of both current members and prospects and both these groups are included in this gender analysis.) Perhaps females in female-dominant work settings perceive a greater sense of challenge or adversity in their work environment, which causes those in the field to find greater value in collective action. But that same adversity may be influencing younger women to avoid the field by finding other career options. A lower distribution of females in the younger age groups may reflect fewer entering the field, which would be the root cause of fewer deciding to join the associations (Exhibit 6.7).

The significance of this demographic distinction carries into the importance women place on the specific activities that lie at the core of their association experience.

EXHIBIT 6.7

Percentages of Females by Age and Gender Setting

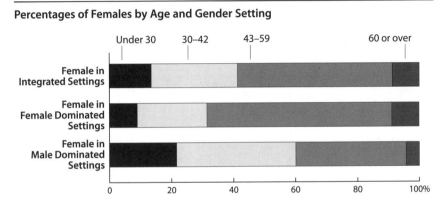

In the category dealing with direct personal benefits, women in female-dominant settings assign significantly higher importance ratings to five of the eight personal benefits. Women in male-dominant settings give a higher importance rating to only one variable (networking) but significantly lower ratings to gaining leadership experience and professional development/education (Exhibit 6.8).

In the category of good-of-the-order benefits, those that provide value for all practitioners regardless of membership status, the seven activities with differences based on gender ratio in the work setting do not line up so neatly with overall importance ranking from all respondents; nor do they appear to contain a unifying theme as may be the case in the personal benefits. Nevertheless, these findings support the point that women in female-dominant settings appear to be far more adamant in expressing the importance of collective action (Exhibit 6.9).

Despite the higher level of loyalty that women in female-dominant settings seem to have for their associations, as well as the higher levels of importance they assign to a majority of the program activities, women in male-dominant associations seem to exert more energy in one area. Asked whether they had volunteered for any association activities in the last year, 29 percent of those in female-dominant organizations report that they had, compared to 38 percent of the female respondents in male dominant associations.

EXHIBIT 6.8

How IMPORTANT were [would be] the following personal benefits in your decision to join?
(Rated on 1-5 scale with 5=very important. Mean rating shown. Asked about a particular association to both members and nonmembers. All ratings are significantly different.)

| | Women: | | | | | |
| | In Integrated Settings | | In Female-Dominant Settings | | In Male-Dominant Settings | |
	Mean	Rank	Mean	Rank	Mean	Rank
Access to the most up to date information available in your field	4.22	1	4.49	1	4.15	1
Professional development or educational program offerings	4.10	2	4.39	2	3.48	4
Opportunities for you to network with other professionals in your field	3.82	3	3.82	3	3.94	2
Access to career information and employment opportunities	3.54	4	3.72	4	3.52	3
Opportunities to gain leadership experience	3.32	5	3.25	6	2.68	7
Access to products, services, and suppliers (e.g. insurance, publications, etc.)	3.24	6	3.47	5	3.10	5
A reference directory of members/ practitioners	3.13	7	3.13	8	2.67	8
Member discounts or group purchasing activities	2.98	8	3.13	7	2.82	6

While respondents answered these questions in reference to a particular association, most associations offer some or all of the personal benefits listed here. All respondents answered questions about the importance of these personal benefits regardless of member status. Women in female-dominant fields give higher ratings to six of the eight benefits. Women in male-dominant settings give higher ratings to the importance of networking and lower ratings for "opportunities to gain leadership experience."

Mean shows the average rating on a 1-5 scale with 5=very important. Rank is the order of priority. "Significant" differences in this and all tables refers to a finding of statistically significant differences based on the application of an appropriate statistical test.

EXHIBIT 6.9

How IMPORTANT were [would be] the following benefits to your field or profession in your decision to join?

(Rated on 1-5 scale with 5=very important. Mean rating shown. Asked about a particular association to both members and nonmembers. All ratings are significantly different.)

	Women:					
	In Integrated Settings		In Female-Dominant Settings		In Male-Dominant Settings	
	Mean	Rank	Mean	Rank	Mean	Rank
Providing standards or guidelines that support quality	3.94	1	4.26	1	3.40	6
Gathering, analyzing, and publishing data on trends in the field	3.85	2	3.93	9	3.66	2
Maintaining a code of ethics for practice	3.82	3	4.23	2	3.28	7
Influencing legislation and regulations that affect the field	3.82	4	4.11	5	3.26	8
Promoting a greater appreciation of the role and value of the field among practitioners	3.79	5	4.14	4	3.41	5
Conducting research on significant issues affecting the field	3.75	6	3.91	10	3.62	3
Promoting greater public awareness of contributions in the field	3.75	7	4.01	6	3.52	4
Certifying those who meet critical competency standards	3.64	8	4.15	3	2.78	12
Attracting competent people into the field	3.57	9	3.95	7	3.24	9
The association's role in defining critical competencies	3.55	10	3.90	11	2.87	11
Supporting student education and entry into the field	3.53	11	3.94	8	3.67	1
Providing awards or recognition for excellence in the field	3.05	12	3.40	12	3.03	10

While respondents answered these questions in reference to a particular association, most associations provide some or all of these benefits to all in their industry or field. All respondents answered questions about the importance of these benefits regardless of member status. As found with their ratings of personal benefits, covered in Exhibit 6.7, women in female-dominant settings give higher ratings on good-of-the-order benefits for every item than do other female respondents.

Mean shows the average rating on a 1-5 scale with 5=very important. Rank is the order of priority. "Significant" differences in this and all tables refers to a finding of statistically significant differences based on the application of an appropriate statistical test.

associations. This is noteworthy at this point because one might logically think that the loyalty and program adamancy might drive a higher rate of volunteerism. It is noteworthy also because many fewer women in male-dominant fields rate gaining leadership experience as "very important" to them in their decision to join an association (Exhibit 6.10).

EXHIBIT 6.10

Female Participation in Any Volunteer Activity in the Last 12 Months

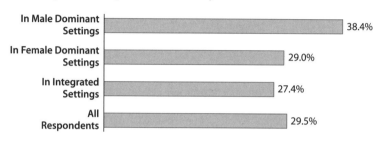

In Male Dominant Settings	38.4%
In Female Dominant Settings	29.0%
In Integrated Settings	27.4%
All Respondents	29.5%

Men by Gender Mix

A comparison of Exhibit 6.5 and Exhibit 6.11 shows that many fewer male respondents are in female-dominant settings than there are women respondents in male-dominated fields.

Creating segments for men based on their workplace and association gender ratio portrays a different picture from that created by women, where affiliations in same-gender fields results in significantly greater value

EXHIBIT 6.11

Distribution of Men by Gender Dominance in Field

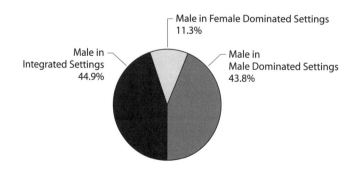

Male in Female Dominated Settings 11.3%

Male in Integrated Settings 44.9%

Male in Male Dominated Settings 43.8%

for their association experience. Men in fields in which their own gender predominates do not show this same gender preference. In fact, men also report higher value for their association experience if they are in female-dominant fields (Exhibit 6.12).

Like their female counterparts, men in female-dominant fields give higher importance ratings for all personal benefits, but rank orders are much more closely aligned with the ratings found among men in integrated fields (Exhibit 6.13). An interesting finding among men in male-dominant fields is the much lower rating they give for "opportunities to gain leadership experience." This is quite an interesting finding, since men in

male-dominant settings were more likely to report volunteering for their association than were men in other associations.

In keeping with the consistent finding that those who work in female-dominant fields find the benefits usually offered by associations more important than do others regardless of gender, men in female-dominant fields rate the importance of all good-of-the-order benefits higher than do men in either integrated or male-dominant fields. (Exhibit 6.14.)

EXHIBIT 6.12

Overarching Value Questions—Men by Gender Mix
(All are significantly different.)

	Men:		
	In Integrated Settings	In Female-Dominant Settings	In Male-Dominant Settings
What is your overall attitude toward associations? *(5-point scale, 5='very favorable')*			
Mean	4.05	4.01	3.98
(% 'very favorable')	34.5%	38.8%	30.8%
Do you believe associations are capable of addressing the practical needs of individual members? *(5-point scale, 5= 'definitely yes')*			
Mean	3.92	3.97	3.74
(% 'definitely yes')	28.1%	35.3%	20.5%
Would you say that there are too many associations in your professional area of interest, too few, or is the number about right?			
Too many	17.5%	11.0%	18.9%
Too few	8.7%	17.1%	7.6%
About right	73.8%	71.9%	73.5%

EXHIBIT 6.12 (continued)

	Men:		
	In Integrated Settings	In Female-Dominant Settings	In Male-Dominant Settings
Do you think there will be a greater or lesser need for associations five years from now?			
Greater	38.2%	51.7%	31.0%
Lesser	11.5%	7.0%	9.9%
About the same	50.4%	41.4%	59.2%
Have you ever dropped membership in any association?			
% Yes	53.1%	52.1%	50.7%
How likely is it that you would recommend membership in [a particular association] to a friend or colleague? *(10-point scale summarized. See* The Ultimate Question *by Fred Reichheld.)*			
Promoter (rating 9 or 10)	42.4%	48.4%	31.3%
Passive (rating 7 or 8)	33.5%	28.2%	37.9%
Detractor (rating 6 or lower)	24.1%	23.5%	30.8%

This table breaks male respondents into three groups: those in "integrated" settings (where men and women are both present), men in female-dominant settings (where women make up 75 percent or more of the field, and men in male-dominant settings (women make up 25 percent or less of the field). Men in male dominant fields, are less positive about their association experience, although somewhat less likely to have dropped an association in the past.

"Significant" differences in this and all tables refers to a finding of statistically significant differences based on the application of an appropriate statistical test.

EXHIBIT 6.13

How IMPORTANT were [would be] the following personal benefits in your decision to join?

(Rated on 1-5 scale with 5=very important. Mean rating shown. Asked about a particular association to both members and nonmembers. All ratings are significantly different.)

| | Men: | | | | | |
| | In Integrated Settings | | In Female-Dominant Settings | | In Male-Dominant Settings | |
	Mean	Rank	Mean	Rank	Mean	Rank
Access to the most up to date information available in your field	4.08	1	4.37	1	4.12	1
Professional development or educational program offerings	3.92	2	4.14	2	3.31	3
Opportunities for you to network with other professionals in your field	3.62	3	3.76	3	3.63	2
Access to career information and employment opportunities	3.23	4	3.46	4	3.14	4
Opportunities to gain leadership experience	3.14	5	3.24	6	2.58	8
Access to products, services, and suppliers (e.g. insurance, publications, etc.)	3.09	6	3.27	5	3.12	5
A reference directory of members/ practitioners	2.95	7	3.10	7	2.61	7
Member discounts or group purchasing activities	2.64	8	3.02	8	2.72	6

While respondents answered these questions in reference to a particular association, most associations offer some or all of the personal benefits listed here. All respondents answered questions about the importance of these personal benefits regardless of member status. Men in female-dominant fields give higher ratings to all of the eight benefits.

Mean shows the average rating on a 1-5 scale with 5=very important. Rank is the order of priority. "Significant" differences in this and all tables refers to a finding of statistically significant differences based on the application of an appropriate statistical test.

EXHIBIT 6.14

How IMPORTANT were [would be] the following benefits to your field or profession in your decision to join?

(Rated on 1-5 scale with 5=very important. Mean rating shown. Asked about a particular association to both members and nonmembers. All ratings are significantly different.)

| | Men: | | | | | |
| | In Integrated Settings | | In Female-Dominant Settings | | In Male-Dominant Settings | |
	Mean	Rank	Mean	Rank	Mean	Rank
Providing standards or guidelines that support quality	3.82	1	4.07	1	3.47	4
Gathering, analyzing, and publishing data on trends in the field	3.70	2	3.93	5	3.63	1
Maintaining a code of ethics for practice	3.70	3	4.00	3	3.33	6
Influencing legislation and regulations that affect the field	3.64	4	3.91	6	3.31	7
Promoting a greater appreciation of the role and value of the field among practitioners	3.58	5	3.87	7	3.59	2
Conducting research on significant issues affecting the field	3.56	6	3.98	4	3.20	9
Promoting greater public awareness of contributions in the field	3.55	7	3.78	10	3.44	5
Certifying those who meet critical competency standards	3.53	8	4.03	2	2.87	12
Attracting competent people into the field	3.44	9	3.82	9	3.00	10
The association's role in defining critical competencies	3.41	10	3.82	8	3.27	8
Supporting student education and entry into the field	3.36	11	3.72	11	3.51	3
Providing awards or recognition for excellence in the field	2.93	12	3.34	12	2.93	11

While respondents answered these questions in reference to a particular association, most associations provide some or all of these benefits to all in their industry or field. All respondents answered questions about the importance of these benefits regardless of member status. As found with their ratings of personal benefits, covered in Exhibit 6.13, men in female-dominant settings give higher ratings on good-of-the-order benefits for every item than do other male respondents.

Mean shows the average rating on a 1-5 scale with 5=very important. Rank is the order of priority. "Significant" differences in this and all tables refers to a finding of statistically significant differences based on the application of an appropriate statistical test.

Chapter Summary

1. When gender ratio in the field is not a factor, meaningful gender differences support the notion that women put greater emphasis on the need to take collective action that will change their environment; men emphasize the need for information regarding the environment in which they find themselves. One implies a stronger need for collective action and the other a stronger need to influence the immediate environment.

2. In a straight comparison of male and female responses, fewer differences exist between men and women than might be expected. The picture changes significantly when the data are considered by gender dominance in the field. When viewed by gender dominance, significant differences appear in the way respondents discern value from associations.

3. Both women and men in female-dominant fields report a significantly greater sense of value of associations in general and assign greater importance to both personal and good-of-the-order benefits offered through a particular association serving their field.

4. Overall, men tend to volunteer more than women, but both men and women in male-dominant settings volunteer at higher rates than they do in integrated or female-dominant settings.

CHAPTER 7

Employer Type and Level of Support

Four employer segments and the extent to which they support memberships through dues payments and the impacts that has on perception of value is examined. The potential for membership growth in these sectors is explored in the context of how these segments differ and the appeals that may work best for each of them. Nonprofits may represent the best prospects. The loyalty and strategic importance of academic members is reflected in the way these respondents appraise their association memberships.

FOUR EMPLOYER TYPES WERE examined to see whether employment environment influences the decision to join: academia, government, nonprofits, and the private sector. As might be expected, this segmentation scheme correlated with significant differences in the way value is perceived.

EXHIBIT 7.1

Respondents by Industry Type

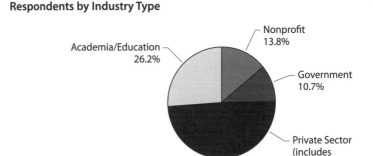

As shown in the overarching value questions (Exhibit 7.2), respondents' status as employees in a nonprofit organization favorably correlated with their perception of the value of associations in general. Some mission-oriented empathy that nonprofits share is one possible reason for this finding. Another explanation might be that individuals in the other sectors

EXHIBIT 7.2

Overarching Value Questions by Employer Type
(All differences are significant.)

	Private Sector	Academia/ Education	Nonprofit	Government
What is your overall attitude toward associations? *(5-point scale, 5='very favorable')*				
Mean	3.99	4.08	4.08	4.01
(% 'very favorable')	32.6%	38.1%	39.6%	36.0%
Do you believe associations are capable of addressing the practical needs of individual members? *(5-point scale, 5='definitely yes')*				
Mean	3.82	3.90	3.95	3.90
(% 'definitely yes')	25.6%	27.2%	31.3%	27.5%
Would you say that there are too many associations in your professional area of interest, too few, or is the number about right? *(No answer excluded.)*				
Too many	14.7%	14.4%	12.5%	15.3%
Too few	10.2%	8.6%	14.0%	8.3%
About right	75.1%	77.0%	73.5%	76.4%
Do you think there will be a greater or lesser need for associations five years from now? *(No answer excluded.)*				
Greater	36.9%	37.3%	45.7%	34.3%
Lesser	9.8%	8.2%	8.2%	7.7%
About the same	53.3%	54.5%	46.0%	57.9%

Those in nonprofit environments are generally more favorable toward associations than others with higher positive attitudes shown in each of the four overarching value questions.

"Significant" differences in this and all tables refers to a finding of statistically significant differences based on the application of an appropriate statistical test.

simply have more demanding expectations. In the private sector, for example, this might be a consequence of working in a more competitive culture that runs on the vaunted concept of ROI (return on investment). In either event, members who work for nonprofits were more positive than respondents in any of the other employment environments.

Academia and government, which are *de facto* nonprofits, follow in order. Respondents from the private sector are the least supportive, particularly on the more substantial question about the delivery of value here and now. When the frame of reference shifts to five years out, government respondents drop to the least supportive position.

Challenges

In the context of this research, a significant difference is not always noteworthy, particularly when it points to a predictable factor. An example of this might include the observation that those in the private sector are more concerned than others with "rapidly changing market conditions" and less concerned with "inadequate sources of funding." Not so apparent but interesting observations might include the fact that private sector respondents are less concerned than others with the challenge of "achieving high-quality outcomes."

Of all the questions asked, environmental challenges will have the highest variability based on the unique conditions of a field. It's therefore not likely that any particular association will find this table to be relevant to their particular situation, but it is worth noting that employer type does account for significant differences in the way challenges in one's professional community are perceived (Exhibit 7.3).

Personal Benefits and Benefits to the Field

In the entire cross tabulation of member segments, employer type shows the least amount of variance on the question of importance of personal benefits. As shown in Exhibit 7.4, the rank order of importance that each segment reports for the personal benefits varies very little.

There is much more variability in importance ratings on good-of-the-order benefits, particularly among those in academia as seen in Exhibit 7.5.

EXHIBIT 7.3

Select the top three challenges that face your professional community.

(Respondents selected up to 3 choices. Significant differences in bold.)

	Private Sector		Academia		Nonprofit		Government	
	%	Rank	%	Rank	%	Rank	%	Rank
Inadequate recognition of the value delivered by the profession or discipline to the larger society	34.5%	1	36.4%	2	32.5%	2	37.3%	1
Keeping up with new information in the field	**32.8%**	**2**	**31.8%**	**3**	**34.7%**	**1**	**29.6%**	**3**
Keeping pace with technology	**26.0%**	**3**	**17.0%**	**7**	**23.3%**	**5**	**25.6%**	**4**
Lack of public awareness of your field	20.8%	4	31.1%	4	22.7%	6	25.1%	5
An expanding body of knowledge	19.1%	5	23.4%	5	20.1%	8	21.3%	7
Inadequate supply of capable professionals	**19.0%**	**6**	**12.4%**	**10**	**23.4%**	**4**	**21.3%**	**6**
Cost containment pressures	18.4%	7	13.2%	8	17.6%	10	14.5%	8
Increasing competition (domestic or international)	**18.1%**	**8**	**9.7%**	**11**	**7.5%**	**15**	**8.0%**	**13**
Challenging regulatory environment (needed relief from regulations)	**16.4%**	**9**	**12.9%**	**9**	**25.7%**	**3**	**9.7%**	**12**
Rapidly changing, difficult to predict market conditions or trends	**15.5%**	**10**	**6.5%**	**15**	**9.4%**	**12**	**7.6%**	**14**
Liability exposure, risk management	**14.9%**	**11**	**6.9%**	**14**	**9.8%**	**11**	**6.9%**	**15**
Inadequate sources of funding or revenue	**13.1%**	**12**	**42.1%**	**1**	**21.0%**	**7**	**32.4%**	**2**
Achieving high-quality outcomes	**13.1%**	**13**	**17.4%**	**6**	**17.7%**	**9**	**13.8%**	**9**
Inadequate supply of support personnel	8.2%	14	9.3%	12	7.9%	13	10.0%	11
Technology replacing practitioners	**7.2%**	**15**	**2.7%**	**16**	**4.7%**	**16**	**10.6%**	**10**
Undesirable pending legislation	6.8%	16	7.9%	13	7.6%	14	5.3%	16

Of all the questions asked, environmental challenges will have the highest variability based on the unique conditions of a field. But, it is worth noting that employer type does account for significant differences in the way professional issues in one's professional community are perceived.

Percent % shows the frequency the item was checked by each type of respondent. Rank is the order of priority. "Significant" differences in this and all tables refers to a finding of statistically significant differences based on the application of an appropriate statistical test.

EXHIBIT 7.4

How IMPORTANT were [would be] the following personal benefits in your decision to join?

(Rated on 1-5 scale with 5=very important. Mean rating shown. Asked about a particular association to both members and nonmembers. Significant differences in bold.)

	Private Sector		Academia		Nonprofit		Government	
	Mean	**Rank**	**Mean**	**Rank**	**Mean**	**Rank**	**Mean**	**Rank**
Access to the most up to date information available in your field	4.16	1	4.26	1	4.35	1	4.23	1
Professional development or educational program offerings	**3.91**	**2**	**3.79**	**3**	**4.18**	**2**	**3.81**	**2**
Opportunities for you to network with other professionals in your field	**3.62**	**3**	**3.86**	**2**	**3.77**	**3**	**3.69**	**3**
Access to career information and employment opportunities	**3.37**	**4**	**3.40**	**4**	**3.66**	**4**	**3.36**	**4**
Access to products, services, and suppliers (e.g. insurance, publications, etc.)	3.20	5	3.22	5	3.30	6	3.20	5
Opportunities to gain leadership experience	**2.98**	**6**	**3.04**	**6**	**3.40**	**5**	**2.86**	**6**
A reference directory of members/ practitioners	**2.91**	**7**	**2.88**	**7**	**3.13**	**8**	**2.88**	**7**
Member discounts or group purchasing activities	**2.79**	**8**	**2.82**	**8**	**3.17**	**7**	**2.83**	**8**

While respondents answered these questions in reference to a particular association, most associations offer some or all of the personal benefits listed here. All respondents answered questions about the importance of these personal benefits regardless of member status. Although there are significant differences in mean ratings, there is little variation in rank order.

Mean shows the average rating on a 1-5 scale with 5=very important. Rank is the order of priority. "Significant" differences in this and all tables refers to a finding of statistically significant differences based on the application of an appropriate statistical test.

Academics are so different in the priority and ratings they assign to good-of-the-order benefits that they are discussed separately in the section following. Other differences are noteworthy as follows:

- In rank ordering, those working for government place the importance of "maintaining a code of ethics for practice" lower than either those in the private sector or in nonprofit organizations. Note, however, that the mean ratings on this benefit are similar for both government and private practice respondents.

- Certification is more important to respondents in nonprofit environments.

Academics as Outliers

To many in association management, academic members are frequently thought of as people with needs and perspectives that mark them as being different. While they are highly revered in some disciplines, such as research-intensive medical specialties, in others they are marginalized by their small numbers and professorial stereotypes that portray them as quirky. In these survey findings they appear to be very predictable in ways that relate to the demands of their employment setting and yet enigmatic in ways that warrant better understanding. Knowing how they determine value in their association context and addressing their needs more effectively can, for some, be a split proposition. They can constitute a small population with peculiar needs that are easily thought of as difficult to justify on a cost-benefit basis. For those who take that point of view these survey findings will challenge the assumptions upon which that opinion is based. Here the academics do come off as being outliers, but they do so in ways that increase their value to associations and in a manner that outweighs their numerical share of the member database.

As seen in Exhibit 7.6, academics are more likely to select five of the nine general association functions as most important. Yet they select the remaining four more frequently than others. This marks them as outliers.

The functions which academics are less likely to select are fairly predictable:

- *Representing the field within the industry or discipline*
- *Creating and disseminating standards of practice*

EXHIBIT 7.5

How IMPORTANT were [would be] the following benefits to your field or profession in your decision to join?

(Rated on 1-5 scale with 5=very important. Mean rating shown. Asked about a particular association to both members and nonmembers. All differences are significant.)

	Private Sector		Academia		Nonprofit		Government	
	Mean	Rank	Mean	Rank	Mean	Rank	Mean	Rank
Providing standards or guidelines that support quality	3.87	1	3.73	5	4.08	1	3.84	1
Maintaining a code of ethics for practice	3.74	2	3.65	7	3.99	2	3.75	5
Gathering, analyzing, and publishing data on trends in the field	3.70	3	3.80	1	3.87	6	3.78	2
Promoting a greater appreciation of the role and value of the field among practitioners	3.68	4	3.67	6	3.92	4	3.71	6
Promoting greater public awareness of contributions in the field	3.59	5	3.76	4	3.85	7	3.76	4
Influencing legislation and regulations that affect the field	3.58	6	3.64	8	3.91	5	3.59	9
Conducting research on significant issues affecting the field	3.58	7	3.77	3	3.83	8	3.76	3
Certifying those who meet critical competency standards	3.55	8	3.31	11	3.95	3	3.47	10
Attracting competent people into the field	3.47	9	3.53	9	3.79	9	3.61	8
Supporting student education and entry into the field	3.43	10	3.78	2	3.78	10	3.67	7
The association's role in defining critical competencies	3.42	11	3.36	10	3.77	11	3.40	11
Providing awards or recognition for excellence in the field	2.94	12	3.18	12	3.33	12	3.18	12

While respondents answered these questions in reference to a particular association, most associations provide some or all of these benefits to all in their industry or field. All respondents answered questions about the importance of these benefits regardless of member status. There are significant differences in all of the ratings and rank order varies considerably for several of these good-of-the-order benefits, particularly in the area of the importance of certification and support for student entry into the field. Most noteworthy are the variations seen among respondents in academia.

Mean shows the average rating on a 1-5 scale with 5=very important. Rank is the order of priority. "Significant" differences in this and all tables refers to a finding of statistically significant differences based on the application of an appropriate statistical test.

• *Providing certification opportunities*
• *Providing training and professional development to members*
• *Providing technical information to members*

These five functions might be thought of as being outside their realm of immediate concerns. The incidence of selecting these functions is not inordinately low, so the functions certainly are of interest to them—but in that classic academic sense, like intellectual spectators looking through a window. The other set of four functions that they select more frequently than other respondents don't fall so easily into a single rationale. They are:

• *Representing the field to the public*
• *Representing the field to the government*
• *Connecting practitioners within the field to each other/networking*
• *Providing timely information about the field to members*

These facts set the stage for conjecture. It may be that academics value the function of "representing the field to the public" because they see it as affecting their discipline's appeal to potential students, which would make it a supply line issue for them. "Representing the field to the government" probably has to do with funding for research or other types of government support programs. But one might have assumed that the private sector's ire over government regulation would be every bit as pressing, and by these findings it is not. "Providing timely information about the field to members" may have to do with the need to maintain awareness of changes in the practice environment that their students are preparing to enter, which by extension may also account for the high rating they give to networking. All this rationalizing may seem plausible, but it nevertheless seems curious that they select all four significantly more frequently than the other segments.

When asked to identify their association memberships, academics are the most likely to report belonging to one or more associations (Exhibit 7.7), which is a positive indicator of the value they see in membership. Academics are also the least likely to report having dropped an association membership (Exhibit 7.8). When they do drop, they tend to do so because "the group was not the right one for me"; they are less apt to report dropping because they change careers and less concerned about activity at the local level (Exhibit 7.8a). Academics are also more likely to volunteer

EXHIBIT 7.6

What do you think are the most important functions of an association?
(Respondents selected up to 3 choices. All are significantly different.)

	Private Sector		Academia		Nonprofit		Government	
	%	Rank	%	Rank	%	Rank	%	Rank
Providing technical information to members	49.9%	1	36.1%	5	37.0%	2	42.7%	1
Providing training/ professional development to members	47.8%	2	40.0%	3	52.0%	1	41.2%	2
Connecting practitioners within the field to each other/ networking	35.2%	3	40.2%	2	30.3%	5	36.4%	4
Creating and disseminating standards of practice	33.6%	4	25.1%	7	33.2%	4	31.1%	5
Providing timely information about the field to members	33.0%	5	44.0%	1	34.0%	3	37.4%	3
Representing the field to the government	24.3%	6	35.1%	6	28.3%	7	25.9%	7
Representing the field to the public	23.0%	7	39.4%	4	22.4%	9	30.8%	6
Representing the field within the industry or discipline	22.6%	8	16.5%	8	22.9%	8	18.8%	9
Providing certification opportunities	20.9%	9	12.5%	9	29.3%	6	20.1%	8

Note how those in academia are the most likely to select four of the functions and least likely to select the other five.

Percent % shows the frequency the item was checked by each type of respondent. Rank is the order of priority. "Significant" differences in this and all tables refers to a finding of statistically significant differences based on the application of an appropriate statistical test.

(Exhibit 7.9). And finally, when asked "the ultimate question," academics are most likely to be the association's biggest promoters (Exhibit 7.10).

One of the lessons learned from these findings is that associations with academic members might want to reconsider their unique value in influencing others—particularly younger individuals—beyond their size in numbers of members. Not all associations marginalize their academic members. As noted earlier, in some they are actually revered. Some professions wish for the day when they might have clearly established degree programs and faculty to cultivate practitioners. And certainly academics rule (and may possibly marginalize practitioners) in some associations based on collegiate disciplines, but it is clear that associations with academic members should consider special outreach to this group. They may be your greatest promoters and most under-appreciated asset.

EXHIBIT 7.7

If you currently belong to any association representing your profession, industry, or field, please name it below.

	Private Sector	Academia/ Education	Nonprofit	Government
% naming any organization	47.3%	59.9%	33.2%	51.6%

EXHIBIT 7.8

Have you ever dropped membership in any association?

	Private Sector	Academia/ Education	Nonprofit	Government
% Yes	52.8%	46.8%	49.9%	55.3%

EXHIBIT 7.8a

[Asked only if respondent ever dropped membership in an association (see Exhibit 7.2)]
Did any of the following play a role in your decision to drop membership in the association you dropped most recently?
(Respondents selected up to five choices. Significant differences in bold.)

	Private Sector		Academia		Nonprofit		Government	
	%	Rank	%	Rank	%	Rank	%	Rank
Did not receive the expected value to justify the cost of dues	56.8%	1	53.9%	1	57.9%	1	56.1%	1
Change of career focus	**26.6%**	**2**	**21.1%**	**3**	**24.7%**	**2**	**24.5%**	**2**
Change of professional interest	19.3%	4	21.3%	2	20.3%	6	20.7%	3
Employer stopped paying membership dues	**18.9%**	**5**	**15.7%**	**7**	**21.7%**	**4**	**18.3%**	**4**
Dissatisfied with association performance	22.2%	3	20.0%	4	21.0%	5	18.1%	5
Not enough local programs offered	**17.3%**	**7**	**14.0%**	**8**	**21.9%**	**3**	**15.5%**	**6**
Change of job	16.8%	8	14.0%	9	17.7%	7	14.0%	7
Association was ineffective in representing your field	18.4%	6	17.8%	5	15.5%	8	13.5%	8
The group was not the right one for me	**14.5%**	**9**	**16.0%**	**6**	**10.8%**	**9**	**12.9%**	**9**
Disagreed with association's political/ advocacy positions	9.3%	11	10.5%	10	7.1%	12	8.6%	10
Dissatisfied with the local chapter	**10.6%**	**10**	**6.7%**	**12**	**9.0%**	**10**	**8.0%**	**11**
Change of residence	9.1%	12	8.5%	11	7.2%	11	7.7%	12
Did not feel welcomed in the group	6.4%	13	5.9%	13	6.9%	13	6.3%	13
Change of local chapter relationship with association	2.4%	14	1.8%	14	2.2%	14	1.9%	14

EXHIBIT 7.9

In the last 12 months, have you volunteered for *[a named association]* in any of the following ways?

(Asked only of current members. Summarized from a list of multiple response options.)

	Private Sector	Academia/ Education	Nonprofit	Government
% Yes	24.0%	48.4%	31.2%	36.0%

EXHIBIT 7.10

How likely is it that you would recommend membership in *[a particular association]* to a friend or colleague?

(Asked only of current members about a particular association. 10-point scale summarized. See The Ultimate Question *by Fred Reichheld.)*

	Private Sector	Academia/ Education	Nonprofit	Government
Promoter (rating 9 or 10)	38.0%	51.0%	45.8%	44.0%
Passive (rating 7 or 8)	32.0%	30.2%	28.4%	32.7%
Detractor (rating 6 or lower)	30.1%	18.9%	25.7%	23.3%

Who Pays Dues

Unfortunately, no baseline exists to support the conviction of numerous association membership directors that the number of employers who pay employee association dues has declined. But both qualitative and quantitative findings among former members responding to this study support that notion.

The notion that employer payment of dues was higher in the past than the overall 42.8 percent found in this study—probably much higher—is based on the frequency of selecting "employer stopped paying dues" among former members when asked why they dropped membership in the past (see Exhibit 4.6). This finding coupled with the number of open-ended comments given to the question dealing with the most important reason for dropping a membership where we see "used to," "doesn't any more," "stopped paying," etc., given as the reason. If these qualitative comments are indicative, it's not a matter of employers who do and don't. It's a collapse of those who used to. The remaining question is: *Has the decline flattened out yet, or is it heading to zero? If so, at what pace?* If this study makes

no other enduring contribution, here stands an important data point: Two thirds of the people who are former members, are not now members of any association, and have been in the past report that their employer does not pay dues for any association (Exhibit 7.12).

The differences in attitudes and opinions found between those whose employers pay association dues and those that don't enjoy this benefit are few.

- In Exhibit 7.13, while differences between the two groups are statistically significant for these items, only one difference is particularly large.

EXHIBIT 7.11

Respondents' Awareness of Employer Willingness to Pay Member Dues for Any Association

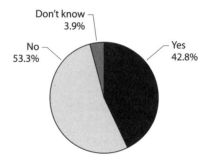

Don't know 3.9%
No 53.3%
Yes 42.8%

EXHIBIT 7.12

Does Employer Pay Dues by Member Status?

- In Exhibit 7.14 we see more and greater differences based on employer payment of dues. These findings reinforce the notion that when individuals pay their own association dues, challenges associated with recognition, public awareness, and funding are greater concerns.

In terms of benefits offered by a particular association, importance ratings for only two personal benefits are significantly different by employer payment of dues. But the rank for both is the same regardless (Exhibit 7.15).

- "Access to products, services, and suppliers (e.g., insurance, publications, etc.)" is more important to respondents whose employer does not pay dues.
- "Opportunities to gain leadership experience" is more important in environments where the employer pays dues.

Again, reinforcing the importance of public awareness and recognition to respondents in environments where the employer does not pay association dues, we see only two significant differences in good-of-the-order benefits (Exhibit 7.16):

- "Promoting greater public awareness of contributions in the field" is rated higher and is located higher in rank ordering among those whose employer does not pay.

EXHIBIT 7.13

What do you think are the most important functions of an association?
(Respondents selected up to 3 choices. Significant differences in bold.)

	Employer Pays Dues		Employer Does Not Pay Dues	
	%	Rank	%	Rank
Providing training/professional development to members	**51.3%**	**1**	**42.2%**	**2**
Providing technical information to members	44.2%	2	42.7%	1
Connecting practitioners within the field to each other/networking	37.7%	3	35.5%	4
Providing timely information about the field to members	36.7%	4	36.8%	3
Creating and disseminating standards of practice	31.0%	5	30.5%	6
Representing the field to the government	26.8%	6	29.1%	7
Representing the field to the public	**23.6%**	**7**	**31.0%**	**5**
Representing the field within the industry or discipline	21.7%	8	20.0%	9
Providing certification opportunities	**17.3%**	**9**	**20.9%**	**8**

Only three of the functions are selected more frequently by those whose employers do not pay dues.

Percent % shows the frequency the item was checked by each type of respondent. Rank is the order of priority. "Significant" differences in this and all tables refers to a finding of statistically significant differences based on the application of an appropriate statistical test.

EXHIBIT 7.14

Select the top three challenges that face your professional community.
(Respondents selected up to 3 choices. Significant differences in bold.)

	Employer Pays Dues		Employer Does Not Pay Dues	
	%	Rank	%	Rank
Keeping up with new information in the field	31.7%	1	32.1%	2
Inadequate recognition of the value delivered by the profession or discipline to the larger society	**31.3%**	**2**	**37.0%**	**1**
Keeping pace with technology	23.6%	3	22.9%	5
Challenging regulatory environment (needed relief from regulations)	**23.1%**	**4**	**12.7%**	**11**
Inadequate sources of funding or revenue	**21.0%**	**5**	**25.8%**	**4**
Lack of public awareness of your field	**20.7%**	**6**	**26.4%**	**3**
Cost containment pressures	**19.0%**	**7**	**15.0%**	**8**
An expanding body of knowledge	19.0%	8	21.2%	6
Increasing competition (domestic or international)	**16.9%**	**9**	**13.0%**	**10**
Inadequate supply of capable professionals	16.7%	10	18.7%	7
Achieving high-quality outcomes	15.5%	11	14.3%	9
Rapidly changing, difficult-to-predict market conditions or trends	**15.1%**	**12**	**9.6%**	**13**
Liability exposure, risk management	**12.4%**	**13**	**10.3%**	**12**
Inadequate supply of support personnel	8.5%	14	8.5%	14
Undesirable pending legislation	7.0%	15	7.1%	16
Technology replacing practitioners	**3.5%**	**16**	**7.6%**	**15**

In this table we see more differences based on employer payment of dues. These findings reinforce the notion that when employers do not pay association dues respondents express greater concern with issues having to do with recognition, public awareness, and funding.

Percent % shows the frequency the item was checked by each type of respondent. Rank is the order of priority. "Significant" differences in this and all tables refers to a finding of statistically significant differences based on the application of an appropriate statistical test.

- "Providing awards or recognition for excellence in the field," while in last place regardless of who pays dues, is rated more highly among those whose employers do not pay.

The importance of employer support for the association industry is seen clearly in the fact that two thirds of those whose employers do not pay dues and were in the co-sponsor nonmember population said they would join today if the employer changed that policy and did provide dues support (see Exhibit B.20 in Appendix B). The implications of this are fairly enormous, particularly when coupled with the previously noted indication that the number of employers willing to pay dues may be in decline. Some individual membership associations have tried to re-craft their value propositions in a way that facilitates a more direct appeal to employers, pointing out how the association is serving the employer's need with respect to activities such as professional development and the career appeal of occupations these employers depend upon. The time may have come for the association profession to move from these fledging initiatives by a few into a more collaborative, assertive, strategic effort by the entire industry.

There are those in association management who over the years have voiced the opinion that people who don't pay for something don't appreciate

EXHIBIT 7.15

How IMPORTANT were [would be] the following personal benefits in your decision to join?

(Rated on 1-5 scale with 5=very important. Mean rating shown. Asked about a particular association to both members and nonmembers. Significant differences in bold.)

	Employer Pays Dues		Employer Does Not Pay Dues	
	Mean	Rank	Mean	Rank
Access to the most up to date information available in your field	4.18	1	4.26	1
Professional development or educational program offerings	3.96	2	3.88	2
Opportunities for you to network with other professionals in your field	3.75	3	3.71	3
Access to career information and employment opportunities	3.37	4	3.45	4
Access to products, services, and suppliers (e.g. insurance, publications, etc.)	**3.15**	**5**	**3.24**	**5**
Opportunities to gain leadership experience	**3.15**	**6**	**2.96**	**6**
Member discounts or group purchasing activities	2.70	8	2.91	7
A reference directory of members/practitioners	2.95	7	2.91	8

While respondents answered these questions in reference to a particular association, most associations offer some or all of the personal benefits listed here. All respondents answered questions about the importance of these personal benefits regardless of member status. Again, consistent with earlier findings there are few differences in the mean importance of ratings given to personal benefits by employer payment of dues. In both cases, however, the rank order is exactly the same.

Mean shows the average rating on a 1-5 scale with 5=very important. Rank is the order of priority. "Significant" differences in this and all tables refers to a finding of statistically significant differences based on the application of an appropriate statistical test.

EXHIBIT 7.16

How IMPORTANT were [would be] the following benefits to your field or profession in your decision to join?

(Rated on 1-5 scale with 5=very important. Mean rating shown. Asked about a particular association to both members and nonmembers. All differences are significant.)

	Employer Pays Dues		Employer Does Not Pay Dues	
	Mean	Rank	Mean	Rank
Providing standards or guidelines that support quality	3.80	1	3.87	1
Gathering, analyzing, and publishing data on trends in the field	3.75	2	3.78	2
Maintaining a code of ethics for practice	3.68	3	3.78	3
Promoting greater public awareness of contributions in the field	**3.55**	**7**	**3.75**	**4**
Promoting a greater appreciation of the role and value of the field among practitioners	3.64	4	3.75	5
Conducting research on significant issues affecting the field	3.63	5	3.74	6
Influencing legislation and regulations that affect the field	3.59	6	3.67	7
Supporting student education and entry into the field	3.50	8	3.66	8
Attracting competent people into the field	3.45	10	3.58	9
Certifying those who meet critical competency standards	3.48	9	3.55	10
The association's role in defining critical competencies	3.41	11	3.47	11
Providing awards or recognition for excellence in the field	**2.99**	**12**	**3.14**	**12**

While respondents answered these questions in reference to a particular association, most associations provide some or all of these benefits to all in their industry or field. All respondents answered questions about the importance of these benefits regardless of member status. Again, few differences but we see again the greater importance given to public awareness among those whose employer does not pay.

Mean shows the average rating on a 1-5 scale with 5=very important. Rank is the order of priority. "Significant" differences in this and all tables refers to a finding of statistically significant differences based on the application of an appropriate statistical test.

it anywhere near as much as those who do. It's offered as a way of reconciling the perceived decline in employer support. With all due respect to that noble ethic, when employers pay it brightens the day for associations, but unfortunately that's not the current forecast. For those who prefer to see a cup half full, the clear and consistent differences between respondents whose employers pay or do not pay dues on the subject of public awareness and recognition should make it easier for membership marketers to fashion messages that will appeal to these individuals.

Chapter Summary

1. Respondents working in nonprofit environments, including government and academia, tend to have a higher estimation of the value associations provide than do those in the private sector.

2. The academic respondents in this survey might be thought of as their associations' most valued members because they
   - Have more association memberships
   - Are the least apt to drop membership once they join
   - Are far more apt to volunteer
   - Are far more apt to be an association promoter, which given their influence over students makes this attribute one of compounding value

3. Two thirds of those who are now members of any association and have dropped an association membership in the past say that their employer stopped paying dues.

4. When employers do not pay dues, respondents are more concerned with challenges associated with public awareness and recognition. There are few other differences between the two conditions.

CHAPTER 8

World Location

What strategic implications emerge when United States-based associations pursue global strategies? Respondents residing outside the United States are remarkably similar to their American colleagues in many ways but distinctly different in some critical respects. The unique considerations that each association faces when it develops a global strategy are beyond the scope of this study. But these findings do illustrate the magnitude of implications that can occur in a United States-based association as the number of global members increases. Infrastructure requirements such as the capacity to provide ad hoc voluntary involvement opportunities are among the factors to consider. The strategic planning impact of program priority ratings systems that reflect member preferences is another.

MANY "AMERICAN" ASSOCIATIONS ARE now considering or actively pursuing global growth strategies for a variety of reasons. In some cases, these reasons have not been adequately explained to domestic members who frequently see these strategies as potentially weakening the association's focus on their needs, or worse, giving global competitors access to association assets that may strengthen their position at the expense of members located in the United States. The failure to explain global initiatives clearly to current members may simply be a communication shortcoming. It may also be a more deeply rooted problem that occurs when an association launches a global strategy without analyzing its motives beyond the common platitudes like "globalization is the future." From the perspective of many who are outside the planning circle, that type of reasoning runs the risk of looking like a junket for leaders who feel they must investigate these prospects through international diplomacy (and travel).

There is no single success strategy for association global initiatives. For example, a scientific society whose members are mainly in an academic setting will have fewer domestic barriers to deal with than one in which a significant portion of the members work in a corporate environment. Factors that go into successful global strategies include clear thinking on the reason why it is being pursued and sound data on the likely consequences it will have for current domestic members. Reasons why associations pursue these strategies include motives such as these:

- Grow the association by expanding its market reach, providing full membership and product and service access on a global scale (expansionist marketing strategy).

- Welcome global members but with the clear understanding that it is an "American" society and will continue to set priorities based on the needs of members located in the United States (respond to demand by sharing, but not changing priorities).

- Accelerate an expanding body of knowledge through global information sharing networks (seamless expansion of a body of knowledge; science-oriented).

- Advance the interests of members in the United States through opening new forums, markets, and policies (advocate on behalf of domestic member interests).

- Assist developing nations by sharing the expertise of United States members (philanthropic).

This study did not address reasons for expansion outside the United States but does shed some light on the consequences that increased membership outside the United States (if that is the goal) might have on an association. The findings from this survey provide a starting point in that investigation by showing why this respondent population might or might not join associations based in the United States and the effect that has on the memberships' estimation of the value they receive from the various programs.

The respondent population residing "inside and outside the United States" is the simplest segmentation scheme looked at in this study. The population residing outside the United States accounts for 2,439 respondents. Exhibit 8.1 shows the distribution of respondents outside the United States by continent. Note that this analysis is devoted to the question of residence, not citizenship, so non-United States citizens residing inside the United States (approximately 2 percent of the United States-based respondents) are included in "United States residents" group and United States expatriates (approximately 6 percent of the "outside United States" group) are included in the "outside United States" group.

If the business of associating is as uniquely American as Tocqueville claimed more than a century ago, one might expect to see United States

EXHIBIT 8.1

Count of Respondents Outside the United States by Continent of Residence

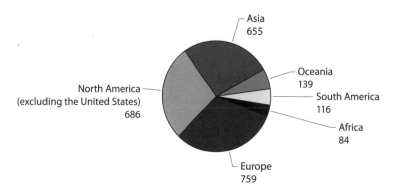

- Asia 655
- Oceania 139
- South America 116
- Africa 84
- Europe 759
- North America (excluding the United States) 686

members having a more positive predisposition toward associations than non-United States respondents. This was not the case. Asked about their overall attitude toward associations, the difference between these two segments is negligible. Asked the more substantial question about the capability of associations in addressing the needs of individual members, the United States respondents are slightly more favorable.

Differences in the rank order of importance for the generic association functions are limited and fairly predictable, as indicated in Exhibit 8.2.

- Training and professional development are—or have been until recently—highly affected by geography or distance from primary United States venues, and it is therefore reasonable to assume that those residing outside the United States would not have this as high on their expectations. This will, however, provide a baseline measure as distance learning vehicles become more prevalent.

- Respondents outside the United States also rank government advocacy lower than United States members, likely because they know their governments are not the targets of the messages being sent by associations based in the United States. But it is interesting to note that they rank public advocacy equal to or higher than their United States counterparts. Both are advocacy programs, but the public is a more amorphous concept than a government. The unanswered question deals with the extent to which public advocacy programs of a

Countries Included from Each Continent

AFRICA	Kenya	Bangladesh	Oman	EUROPE	Ireland	Spain	Cayman	Saint Vincent	SOUTH
Algeria	Nigeria	Burma	Pakistan	Albania	Italy	Sweden	Islands	and The	AMERICA
Angola	Rwanda	**China**	Philippines	Austria	Latvia	Switzerland	Costa-Rica	Grenadines	Argentina
Benin	South Africa	East Timor	Qatar	Belarus	Lithuania	Ukraine	Cuba	St. Kitts and	Bolivia
Botswana	Sudan	Georgia	Saudi Arabia	Belgium	Malta	**United**	Dominican	Nevis	Brazil
Burkina-Faso	Swaziland	**India**	Singapore	Bulgaria	Moldova	**Kingdom**	Republic	Trinidad and	Chile
Burundi	Tanzania	Indonesia	Taiwan	Croatia	Monaco	Vatican City	El Salvador	Tobago	Colombia
Central	Tunisia	Iran	Tajikistan	Czech	Netherlands		Grenada		Ecuador
African	Western	Israel	Thailand	Republic	Norway	NORTH	Guatemala	OCEANIA	Guyana
Republic	Sahara	**Japan**	Turkey	Denmark	Poland	AMERICA	Honduras	**Australia**	Peru
Congo	Zambia	Jordan	Turkmenistan	Estonia	Portugal	Anguilla	Jamaica	Cook Islands	Uruguay
Cote-d'Ivoire	Zimbabwe	Kazakhstan	United Arab	Finland	Romania	Antigua and	**Mexico**	Micronesia	Venezuela
Dem. Republic		Korea, South	Emirates	France	Russia	Barbuda	Nicaragua	New Zealand	
of Congo	ASIA	Kuwait	Uzbekistan	**Germany**	Serbia and	Bahamas	Panama	Tuvalu	Highlighted
Egypt	Afghanistan	Lebanon	Vietnam	Greece	Montenegro	Bermuda	Saint Lucia	Vanuatu	countries are those
Gabon	Armenia	Malaysia	Yemen	Hungary	Slovakia	**Canada**			from which 100 or
Ghana	Azerbaijan	Mongolia		Iceland	Slovenia				more responses were received.

EXHIBIT 8.2

What do you think are the most important functions of an association?
(Respondents selected up to 3 choices. Significant differences in bold.)

	USA		Outside USA	
	%	Rank	%	Rank
Providing training/professional development to members	**49.6%**	**1**	**35.8%**	**4**
Providing technical information to members	**42.0%**	**2**	**49.2%**	**1**
Providing timely information about the field to members	**35.3%**	**3**	**43.9%**	**2**
Connecting practitioners within the field to each other/ networking	**34.7%**	**4**	**41.4%**	**3**
Creating and disseminating standards of practice	**31.3%**	**5**	**27.6%**	**6**
Representing the field to the government	**30.0%**	**6**	**19.4%**	**8**
Representing the field to the public	26.9%	7	29.9%	5
Providing certification opportunities	**20.8%**	**8**	**15.0%**	**9**
Representing the field within the industry or discipline	20.2%	9	21.6%	7

Training and professional development benefits were not as important to global respondents. Yet they rate networking as being more important than United States respondents.

Percent % shows the frequency the item was checked by each type of respondent. Rank is the order of priority. "Significant" differences in this and all tables refers to a finding of statistically significant differences based on the application of an appropriate statistical test.

United States-based association will reach their local public or if they are seeking to influence the United States market.

As shown in Exhibit 8.3, preferences for how they wish to receive information about their field or profession are nearly identical. Respondents in the United States note a somewhat greater preference for e-newsletters than do those outside the United States. Real differences, however, are found in the incidence of preference for the Internet, although rank order is the same for both groups.

The marginal differences between these segments when comparing generic functions of associations (Exhibit 8.2) do not carry over to the comparison of their differences on the perception of challenges facing their professional community (Exhibit 8.4). Although the degree of difference between these two segments is fairly substantial in both the frequency of selecting the challenges and their rank, it is difficult to see a pattern or rationale that might account for the differences until we look at their demographic characteristics.

As shown in Exhibit 8.8, the demographic differences between these two segments might account for this disparity. Respondents residing outside the United States include a significantly greater percentage of academic members, which may account for several of the differences, discussed in more detail in Chapter 7, "Employer Type." Respondents in academia indicate higher importance for information on the field, less concern for keeping up with technology, and more concern for adequate funding. On the other hand, the greater emphasis that global members place on achieving quality outcomes and increasing competition correlate more strongly with those in the private sector.

EXHIBIT 8.3

How do you prefer to receive information about your profession or field?
(Respondents selected up to 3 choices. Significant differences in bold.)

	USA		Outside USA	
	%	Rank	%	Rank
In magazines or journals serving your field	65.2%	1	63.3%	1
At conferences or meetings	54.4%	2	51.2%	2
In E-newsletters	**54.3%**	**3**	**48.1%**	**3**
Through an association Web site	47.9%	4	44.6%	4
By searching on the Internet	**15.2%**	**5**	**24.9%**	**5**
Through your network of peers (word of mouth)	12.8%	6	10.5%	7
Through communities of practice (e.g. special interest groups, user groups, etc.)	11.5%	7	13.4%	6
In print sources other than magazines or newspapers	6.6%	8	5.6%	9
In general interest magazines	3.4%	9	6.2%	8
In newspapers (print)	2.9%	10	4.5%	10
Through traditional broadcast media (television or radio)	1.7%	11	1.7%	12
Through blogs or podcasts	1.7%	12	3.3%	11

There are only two significant differences in information delivery preferences and no differences in rank order of preference for information delivery by global location.

Percent % shows the frequency the item was checked by each type of respondent. Rank is the order of priority. "Significant" differences in this and all tables refers to a finding of statistically significant differences based on the application of an appropriate statistical test.

EXHIBIT 8.4

Select the top three challenges that face your professional community.
(Respondents selected up to 3 choices. Significant differences in bold.)

	USA		Outside USA	
	%	Rank	%	Rank
Inadequate recognition of the value delivered by the profession or discipline to the larger society	**35.5%**	**1**	**28.0%**	**2**
Keeping up with new information in the field	32.2%	2	32.4%	1
Lack of public awareness of your field	**24.7%**	**3**	**20.8%**	**7**
Keeping pace with technology	**24.0%**	**4**	**20.7%**	**8**
Inadequate sources of funding or revenue	22.7%	5	25.5%	4
Challenging regulatory environment (needed relief from regulations)	**19.4%**	**6**	**9.0%**	**12**
An expanding body of knowledge	**18.6%**	**7**	**26.2%**	**3**
Inadequate supply of capable professionals	17.5%	8	18.1%	9
Cost containment pressures	17.1%	9	14.9%	10
Increasing competition (domestic or international)	**13.2%**	**10**	**20.9%**	**6**
Liability exposure, risk management	**12.9%**	**11**	**7.3%**	**14**
Achieving high-quality outcomes	**12.8%**	**12**	**22.4%**	**5**
Rapidly changing, difficult to predict market conditions or trends	11.4%	13	13.4%	11
Inadequate supply of support personnel	8.5%	14	8.9%	13
Undesirable pending legislation	**8.1%**	**15**	**2.8%**	**16**
Technology replacing practitioners	6.4%	16	4.3%	15

Differences in perceived challenges facing their professional community are more frequently noted by respondents inside the United States than to those outside. Global respondents' stress on expanding the body of knowledge and achieving high-quality outcomes may have more to do with the high incidence of academic respondents found in this group (see also Exhibit 8.8).

Percent % shows the frequency the item was checked by each type of respondent. Rank is the order of priority. "Significant" differences in this and all tables refers to a finding of statistically significant differences based on the application of an appropriate statistical test.

Personal Benefits

On the question of the importance of personal benefits in the decision to join, the two groups are very much alike (Exhibit 8.5).

Statistically, difference in the mean importance rating for professional development is significant and worth noting. Respondents outside the United States are less concerned with association educational offerings than domestic residents, and this is consistent with the way they rate the generic association functions as shown in Exhibit 8.2. Again, proximity to educational offerings is likely responsible for this disparity. Proximity, however, does not dampen the importance they assign to networking. Other than this, the two segments are similar in the way they rank personal benefits.

How IMPORTANT were [would be] the following personal benefits in your decision to join?
(Rated on 1-5 scale with 5=very important. Mean rating shown. Significant differences in bold. Asked about a particular association to both members and nonmembers. Significant differences in bold.)

	USA		Outside USA	
	Mean	Rank	Mean	Rank
Access to the most up to date information available in your field	**4.20**	**1**	**4.31**	**1**
Professional development or educational program offerings	**4.00**	**2**	**3.61**	**3**
Opportunities for you to network with other professionals in your field	3.74	3	3.67	2
Access to career information and employment opportunities	**3.44**	**4**	**3.14**	**5**
Access to products, services and suppliers (e.g. insurance, publications, etc.)	**3.19**	**5**	**3.30**	**4**
Opportunities to gain leadership experience	3.08	6	3.00	6
A reference directory of members/practitioners	2.96	7	2.84	8
Member discounts or group purchasing activities	2.84	8	2.92	7

While respondents answered these questions in reference to a particular association, most associations offer some or all of the personal benefits listed here. All respondents answered questions about the importance of these personal benefits regardless of member status. Again, professional development is less important to respondents outside the United States, while access to both information about the field (as distinct from career information) and access to products are more important.

Mean shows the average rating on a 1-5 scale with 5=very important. Rank is the order of priority. "Significant" differences in this and all tables refers to a finding of statistically significant differences based on the application of an appropriate statistical test.

Benefits to Field

The comparison swings back to one of distinctly different profiles with respect to the way these segments rank benefits to the field (Exhibit 8.6). Most of these rating differences make perfect sense but are worth considering closely if growth outside the United States is a strategic objective. For example:

- Providing standards that support quality are lower in importance for those residing outside the United States, probably because the global influence of United States standards vary greatly, particularly as unified European-based standard setting organizations grow in influence.

- Maintaining a code of ethics is also less important to those outside the United States, almost certainly due to extreme variation in the way nations frame and enforce ethics.

- Influencing legislation is less important, likely because it is specific to one nation, though some associations have or are developing global advocacy capability with respect to laws and regulations.

EXHIBIT 8.6

How IMPORTANT were [would be] the following benefits to your field or profession in your decision to join?

(Rated on 1-5 scale with 5=very important. Mean rating shown. Significant differences in bold. Asked about a particular association to both members and nonmembers. Significant differences in bold.)

	USA		Outside USA	
	Mean	**Rank**	**Mean**	**Rank**
Providing standards or guidelines that support quality	**3.90**	**1**	**3.68**	**3**
Maintaining a code of ethics for practice	**3.83**	**2**	**3.44**	**7**
Influencing legislation and regulations that affect the field	**3.78**	**3**	**3.16**	**11**
Gathering, analyzing, and publishing data on trends in the field	3.77	4	3.78	1
Promoting a greater appreciation of the role and value of the field among practitioners	**3.77**	**5**	**3.47**	**5**
Promoting greater public awareness of contributions in the field	**3.71**	**6**	**3.53**	**4**
Conducting research on significant issues affecting the field	3.70	7	3.72	2
Supporting student education and entry into the field	**3.62**	**8**	**3.42**	**8**
Certifying those who meet critical competency standards	**3.60**	**9**	**3.28**	**9**
Attracting competent people into the field	**3.56**	**10**	**3.45**	**6**
The association's role in defining critical competencies	**3.50**	**11**	**3.26**	**10**
Providing awards or recognition for excellence in the field	3.06	12	3.12	12

While respondents answered these questions in reference to a particular association, most associations provide some or all of these benefits to all in their industry or field. All respondents answered questions about the importance of these benefits regardless of member status. Many more differences between United States and global respondents are found in these good-of-the-order benefits than in personal benefits. Most of these benefits are rated more important to domestic respondents than they are to global respondents; "gathering, analyzing and publishing data" and "conducting research" are equivalent.

Mean shows the average rating on a 1-5 scale with 5=very important. Rank is the order of priority. "Significant" differences in this and all tables refers to a finding of statistically significant differences based on the application of an appropriate statistical test.

Volunteering

It may come as no surprise to those in associations with a substantial number of members located outside the United States, but it may to those who do not, that outside-United States members volunteer at a slightly higher rate than domestic members.

However, the nature of their volunteer activity is significantly different. As shown in Exhibit 8.7, those who reported volunteering in the past year were more likely to report ad hoc volunteer participation (speaking, writing, presenting, or reviewing content). But many more of the respondents outside the United States reported this type of volunteer activity in the past year than those inside the United States who were more likely to report governance- or committee-level volunteering. (See also Exhibit B.12 in Appendix B). This finding strongly supports the need for associations that identify growth outside the United States as a strategic objective to offer myriad ad hoc opportunities for volunteer involvement.

EXHIBIT 8.7

Types of Volunteer Activity by Location

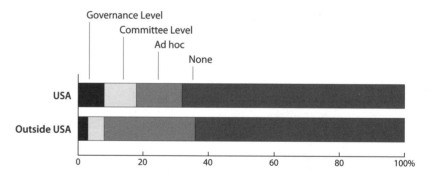

Demographics

Perhaps of greatest value to associations considering an expansion of their international membership are the differences in the demographic characteristics of non-United States respondents. (See Exhibits 8.8 through 8.11.) Focusing on demographics can help associations to market more effectively.

- By a very substantial margin, global respondents are affiliated with academic institutions. The unique characteristics of respondents in the academic environment are discussed in Chapter 7 and should be helpful in designing appeals to this subgroup.

- The career stages of respondents outside the United States (which also reflects age) is very similar to that of the domestic respondents, with the only significant difference being a greater percentage of senior-level people for the global segment, which is offset by a smaller percentage of mid-level folks. No differences are found between the segments with respect to the entry-level people and CEOs.

- Respondents outside the United States are disproportionately male, and this is the most substantial gender difference seen in any of the *segment* comparisons.

- Global members are less apt to be promoters of their association than their domestic colleagues, and nothing in the survey findings indicates why. It may be because key benefits such as professional development opportunities do not reach them as effectively. On a very different note, it could also reflect the fact that they do not believe that peers in their immediate proximity are in a position to rationalize the cost of a membership in an association based in the United States, which would not suggest any criticism of the association's value. There may be support for another view in the fact that the margin of difference at the promoter level is accounted for largely among those who are passive rather than detractors.

EXHIBIT 8.8

Which of the following best describes the type of organization in which you are employed?

	USA	Outside USA
Private Sector	50%	45%
Academic	23%	38%
Nonprofit	17%	4%
Government	10%	13%

EXHIBIT 8.9

Which best describes your current career situation?
(Excludes academia, unemployed, self employed and retired)

	USA	Outside USA
Entry level	6%	6%
Mid level	49%	43%
Senior level	39%	45%
Chief Executive	6%	6%

EXHIBIT 8.10

What is your gender?

	USA	Outside USA
Male	48%	79%
Female	52%	21%

EXHIBIT 8.11

How likely is it that you would recommend membership in [a particular association] to a friend or colleague?
(Asked only of current members about a particular association. 10-point scale summarized. See The Ultimate Question *by Fred Reichheld.)*

	USA	Outside USA
Promoter (rating 9 or 10)	45%	35%
Passive (rating 7 or 8)	30%	37%
Detractor (rating 6 or lower)	25%	28%

Chapter Summary

From a strategic standpoint, one of the most important considerations that an association's leadership should take into account when considering growth outside the United States is in understanding the way this population will change the association's priorities. Every association will have its own profile on this, but these findings give an indication of the influence global members will have.

One of the more distinguishing attributes of the respondents residing outside the United States is that networking is high on their list of important benefits despite the reasonable inclination to think that distance might inhibit this. Furthermore, they show a stronger tendency to volunteer, which validates the importance of networking but raises the issue of viability because distance is a factor. This adds greater emphasis to a point made in Chapter 4, "Affiliation and Involvement." Namely, associations should make a concerted effort to expand the number of ad hoc involvement opportunities, particularly activities that can be accomplished electronically. It doesn't match the networking value of face-to-face, but it enhances the prospects of that happening and the benefits received when it does.

1. Global respondents show no difference in their predisposition toward associations in general. Given that a distinguishing feature of Americans has historically been thought to include a tendency to join voluntary organizations, global respondents to this survey may be unique in that they differ from their peers in their own country on this point. If true, it would mean that current global respondents may not provide accurate information on what it would take to recruit their peers.

2. Training and professional development benefits were not as important to global respondents. While this may be influenced by distance, this conclusion is mitigated by the fact that they rate networking as being more important than do United States respondents.

3. The importance of networking to global members and the reality of their distance from most activities may indicate the need for associations to increase ad hoc volunteer opportunities. The importance of this is elevated further by virtue of the fact that global members are more likely to volunteer for this kind of activity.

4. Global members rank government advocacy lower than do United States members, presumably because they know their governments are not the targets of these initiatives. But it is interesting to note that they rank public advocacy equal to or higher than their United States counterparts. Both are advocacy programs, but the public is a more amorphous concept and population than a government. The unresolved issue is in the extent to which global members think the public advocacy programs of a United States association will or should reach their local public.

5. Maintaining a code of ethics is less important to global members, almost certainly due to extreme variations in the way different nations frame and enforce ethics. The influence of more than 2,000 global respondents on the rank order of importance for ethics was likely to have substantially dropped the importance of this good-of-the-order benefit. This illustrates the significance global members can have on the calculation of member-driven priorities.

6. By a very substantial margin, global respondents have a higher employer affiliation with academic institutions. The extent to which this is a unique attribute of this survey population or a possible indication that academics residing outside the United States are more inclined to seek global networks is not clear but may be noteworthy with respect to future research.

7. Global respondents are disproportionately male, the most substantial gender difference seen in any of the segment comparisons.

CHAPTER 9

Epilogue

I T HAS BEEN SAID that good research raises one's knowledge to a higher level of ignorance. That means there are two metrics on the value of this study. What did it contribute and what questions did it raise?

Fundamentally, this study contributed a research breakthrough by pooling the populations of many associations and establishing more useful definitions of current, former, and never members. Other significant methodological contributions include the distinction made between attitudes toward associations in general versus a specific association in the respondents' field, the importance of environmental challenges as compared to association capabilities, and the extent to which the size of the response database allowed for segmenting into smaller comparison cells.

Opinions on the most significant findings will vary according to readers' interests and the situation of their respective associations, but several do appear to have some universal importance. First among them might be the ability to index the balance of personal and collective benefits that characterize the unique value proposition of any association. Documenting how perilously close uninvolved members are to former members in their estimation of value and the critical segue that ad hoc volunteers provide longer-term involvement may be another. Insights on why it takes entry-level people so long to discover the value of associations and the way they differ from those in other career stages with respect to their benefit ratings should help close a critical gap in recruiting new members. The strategic implications of expanding an association based in the United States to include members outside the United States may only open the door to an area that needs much more attention, but it is an opening that raises the most important question: What's next?

Candidates for future analysis should emerge from the discussions that we hope to stimulate and capture as a consequence of this study. Since this study looked only at individual membership associations, the reasoning and more complicated decision-making dynamics involved in joining a trade association may be the next logical choice. Tocqueville's illustrations of how associations contribute to the common good were replete with trade associations that facilitate commerce in a much more efficient manner than government is one indication that the balance between individual company gain and the good of the industry is relevant. (This may also constitute an important message for the Federal Trade Commission to hear.)

In the research literature, the phrase *persistence and commitment* is given to account for the drivers that motivate people to get involved and the expectations they expect to gain from that involvement. The list of activities used in this study to allow respondents to characterize their voluntary involvement was not, in retrospect, as useful as it might have been. Given the importance that involvement appears to have for the member's level of commitment, more insight in this area may also warrant priority consideration.

The ability of ASAE & The Center for Association Leadership to form research collaborations on these and other topics may be sufficiently appealing to draw academic researchers in fields such as psychology and nonprofit management into this research agenda. The extent to which individuals seek association memberships for reasons having to do with things such as self esteem, locus of control, or ideological beliefs would require a combination of academic expertise and association resources.

In contrast to the way this study merged individual membership associations with care given to creating a diverse array of professions and disciplines, there may be value in research that focuses on categorical differences in types of missions or purpose-related characteristics. Every association has a unique profile with respect to the relative importance of such things as professional development and legislative advocacy. Another dimension of difference is the extent to which associations focus strictly on member interests or the public good as they relate to what their members do.

As an extension of this study we offer several opportunities to leverage the usefulness of this information. A do-it-yourself package is offered to support associations that wish to conduct The Decision to Join study on their own or through their service provider. Godspeed! As an option, ASAE & The Center for Association Leadership staff will conduct the survey as a turnkey service with two goals in mind. The first will be to provide associations with a useful research service, and the second will be to build the pool of normative data. Across time, as the database becomes richer, subsets can be created to profile the decision-making norms in fields and disciples that develop a critical mass of data, such as healthcare, education, and science and engineering. On that note, the 18 associations that are identified and thanked in the Acknowledgements of this book are to be thanked again for their collaboration, which one hopes provided them with institutional benefits as it certainly contributed to the good of the order.

The Decision to Join Study Methodology

THE DECISION TO JOIN study was designed as a coalition of individual membership associations to study their members' and nonmembers' reasons for joining or not joining associations. Eighteen organizations contributed more than 120,000 names of individuals randomly selected from their member and prospect lists. Each individual selected from these lists was qualified to join the contributing organization, and most belonged to at least one other organization.

The 18 organizations that participated in the study represent a diverse group of individual membership organizations whose members do not have to join in order to practice in their profession or field. Since we intended to use the results of the study to generalize about the individual—not about a particular association—it was important to ensure that a wide variety of organizations contribute names. The following organizations cosponsored the study:

- American Chemical Society
- American College of Healthcare Executives
- American Geophysical Union
- American Health Information Management Association
- American Society for Quality
- American Society of Civil Engineers
- American Society of Mechanical Engineers
- College of American Pathologists
- Credit Union Executives Society
- Emergency Nurses Association
- IEEE
- Institute of Food Technologists
- National Association of Secondary School Principals
- National Athletic Trainers Association
- National Court Reporters Association
- National Society of Accountants
- Project Management Institute
- School Nutrition Association

Each participating organization paid a fee to participate in the study and, in return, received a report summarizing data for its organization against all respondents. But this analysis by organization, while a value to the individual co-sponsor, was not used in the preparation of this book. When we discuss "members" and "nonmembers" in this publication, we are referring to individuals who belong or do not belong to any individual membership organization, not in the context of the particular organization that contributed their name.

Sampling Design: Selecting the Individuals Invited

The Decision to Join study was designed for individual membership organizations that must compete for members. The study was administered to members and nonmembers concurrently.

Each co-sponsoring organization submitted a list of between 2,000 and 8,600 names randomly selected from the member and prospect databases. The number of names selected was determined by the organization's historical response rate statistics to achieve at least 300 responses to each version of the questionnaire (see "Instrumentation: Questionnaires and Invitation to Participate," which follows).

A total of 120,540 individuals were sent an invitation to participate. A total of 16,944 responses were received, an average 15 percent response rate. This very large sample size results in overall survey confidence at 99 percent with reliability of plus or minus 1 percent. Confidence is the probability that the sample represents the population and reliability is the interval around which results are accurate. It also allows for high reliability among the subgroups that were examined in the various chapters.

Instrumentation: Questionnaires and Invitation to Participate

Two versions of the questionnaire were prepared and administered depending on an individual's current relationship to the contributing co-sponsor.

Questions 1 through 11 in both the member and nonmember versions of the survey are the same and generic, referring to associations in general, not any organization in particular. This series of questions provides information about the individual's attitude toward the role and function of associations.

Following question 11 in both the nonmember and member versions of the questionnaire, respondents are directed to questions referring to a particular organization. For questions having to do with the importance of various association functions in general, it was necessary to give the respondent a referent association. But again, care was taken to make the questions sufficiently broad, covering the benefits and services offered by most associations, regardless of the industry or field represented. Thus, when looked at in the aggregate across all of the disparate organizations that contributed names for the study, we could make generalizations about associations as a group.

Survey instrumentation also encompassed the following:

- Cover letter (or email depending on data collection method selected—see below)
- Follow-up reminder letter or email
- Postage-paid return envelope for mail data collection
- A follow-up postcard sent to low-response segments

Data Collection: Getting the Responses Back

This study was designed for either Internet or postal mail distribution. All but one of the organizations selected Internet administration.

One original invitation was sent during November 2006 with one follow-up deployment one month later. Initial deployments occurred between November 8th and 20th, 2006. Follow-up deployments occurred four weeks after the first deployment. Segments that did not achieve a minimum of 300 responses after six weeks were sent a follow-up postcard in the postal mail. A total of 34,050 postcards were sent. The postcard was found to be ineffective in increasing response rate.

A response incentive of a drawing for one of three American Express gift cards was offered in the amount of $500.

Data collection was closed on December 31, 2006.

Data Processing: Managing the Response Database

Responses were downloaded and reviewed several times in the first two weeks of the deployment to ensure that data collection and skip patterns were working properly.

Inappropriate or incomplete responses were identified in periodic visual review and removed from the study database. An incomplete was removed when more than half of the questions were left unanswered.

Missing responses were recoded as needed to differentiate between responses that were legitimately skipped (due to contingent questions) and those that the respondent did not answer but should have (no answer). Both no answer and missing were excluded from the tables.

Open-ended responses were classified using SPSS text analysis software.

A number of post-data collection variables were created in The Decision to Join database, including

- Generation based on year born
- World location based on responses to citizenship and residency
- Governance versus other types of volunteer
- Member status (never members and former members) in relation to membership in *any* association

Decision to Join Benchmarking Opportunities

As a companion to the book, we have provided Appendix D containing a step-by-step guide to conducting The Decision to Join for your organization. Through it we are hoping to significantly increase the size of The Decision to Join database and promote the practice of conducting normative research of this type. Organizations choosing to conduct the study on their own are encouraged to contribute their data to this large database to help to advance knowledge about why individuals join membership organizations.

Knowing more about what motivates people to join or not join individual membership organizations will help all membership organizations to target the most compelling membership appeal and spot trends across time.

As an incentive for organizations to provide their results to ASAE & The Center's database, we will provide ad hoc telephone consultation free of charge to organizations conducting the study in-house or using an outside consultant. This will include specific guidance on all of the tasks necessary to complete this study. If SPSS is used for analysis, we will also provide our file structure parameters and the syntax files necessary to create new variables and generate cross-tabulated tables.

This complementary telephone consultation will only be available for organizations that provide information in the appropriate format and allow their data to be added to our Decision to Join database.

Additional analysis can also be provided on a fee-for-service basis. Fee-for-service options include:

- Basic analysis of your data, return of your tables in an Excel file benchmarked against the original database
- Creation of new variables for generation, world location, member status (more finely tuned than member and nonmember), gender-dominant profession or field, and volunteer level
- Statistical tests of significance by any of the key demographics
- Written narrative reports of findings

We also offer a turnkey service for The Decision to Join in which we will conduct the survey on behalf of your organization. This service includes the following:

- A statistically valid survey of your organization's members and nonmembers
- Uniform questions for all co-sponsoring organizations, but early co-sponsors will have the opportunity to include two custom questions
- Custom statistical report benchmarking results for your organization against other professional organizations in the study
- A database of responses for your organization

The following materials can be downloaded from **www.asaecenter.org/decisiontojoin** at a package price:

- Decision to Join questionnaires: templates for the member and nonmember version of The Decision to Join. These templates are also available for electronic implementation.
- Samples of the cover letters and emails used for the invitation to participate in the survey
- Microsoft Excel column format requirements
- Excel report template

Frequency Tables for All Questions/All Respondents

T HE FOLLOWING TABLES PROVIDE the response to all questions asked in the study by all respondents. These tables are the reference guide for all segmentation analysis covered in this book. Chapter 3 covers the rationale for question construction in more detail.

In Part One of the questionnaire, a series of questions about associations in general were asked of everyone who responded in this study, regardless of their relationship to a study co-sponsor as a member, former member or never member. These responses are covered in Tables B.1 through B.8.

Part Two of the questionnaire covered questions in the context of a particular co-sponsor. As discussed in Chapter 3, care was taken to ensure that the questions were generic so that generalizations could be made from a particular association to create a norm. All respondents, regardless of their current relationship to a particular co-sponsor (as a member, former member or never member) answered questions in Part Three as appropriate to their status. The constituency addressed in each of the questions is described in Tables B.9 through B.21.

Closing questions covered demographic characteristics of all respondents.

Part One: About Associations in General

The following questions were asked of all respondents about associations in general. The term "association" in all questions in this study refers to any scientific, scholarly, academic, or professional organization comprised of individual members who seek to benefit from collective activities such as education, networking, or advocacy.

EXHIBIT B.1

What is your overall attitude toward associations as defined above?
(Rated on a scale of 1 to 5 with 5='Very Favorable')

	%
Very Unfavorable (1)	2.5
2	3.7
3	16.7
4	39.6
Very Favorable (5)	34.5
No opinion	*2.9*
	100.0
Mean Rating (No opinion excluded)	**4.03**

EXHIBIT B.2

Do you believe associations are capable of addressing the practical needs of individual members?
(Rated on a scale of 1 to 5 with 5='Definitely Yes')

	%
1 (Definitely No)	0.8
2	6.9
3	22.3
4	40.2
5 (Definitely Yes)	26.5
Can't Say	*3.2*
	100.0
Mean Rating (Can't say excluded)	**3.88**

EXHIBIT B.3

What do you think are the most important functions of an association?
(Respondents selected up to 3 choices. Shown in order with most frequently selected first.)

	%
Providing training/professional development to members	46.4
Providing technical information to members	43.2
Providing timely information about the field to members	36.9
Connecting practitioners within a field to each other/networking	36.7
Creating and disseminating standards of practice	30.8
Representing the field to the public	27.1
Representing the field to the government	27.0
Representing the field within the industry or discipline	20.6
Providing certification opportunities	19.5
Other	*1.7*

EXHIBIT B.4

How do you prefer to receive information about your profession or field?
(Respondents selected up to 3 choices. Shown in order with most frequently selected first.)

	%
In magazines or journals serving your field	63.6
At conferences or meetings	53.3
In E-newsletters	52.3
Through an association Web site	47.4
By searching on the Internet	17.6
Through your network of peers (word of mouth)	12.5
Through communities of practice (e.g. special interest groups, user groups, etc.)	11.9
In print sources other than magazines or newspapers	6.7
In general interest magazines	4.0
In newspapers (print)	3.3
Through blogs or podcasts	2.0
Through traditional broadcast media (television or radio)	1.9
Other	*0.9*

EXHIBIT B.5

Please select the top three challenges that face your professional community. Then rate how well associations address the challenge.

(Respondents selected up to 3 choices. Shown in order with most frequently selected first.)

	%	Mean Rating (1-5 Scale with 5=Very Well)
Inadequate recognition of the value delivered by the profession or discipline to the larger society	33.2%	3.16
Keeping up with new information in the field	32.1%	3.87
Keeping pace with technology	23.6%	3.68
Lack of public awareness of your field	23.5%	2.81
Inadequate sources of funding or revenue	23.3%	2.57
An expanding body of knowledge	20.0%	3.74
Inadequate supply of capable professionals	17.2%	2.78
Challenging regulatory environment (needed relief from regulations)	17.0%	3.36
Cost containment pressures	16.8%	2.69
Achieving high-quality outcomes	15.1%	3.39
Increasing competition (domestic or international)	14.9%	2.91
Rapidly changing, difficult to predict market conditions or trends	12.4%	3.16
Liability exposure, risk management	11.6%	3.13
Inadequate supply of support personnel	8.5%	2.63
Undesirable pending legislation	7.1%	3.47
Technology replacing practitioners	6.1%	3.21

EXHIBIT B.6

Have you ever dropped membership in an association?

	%
Yes	52.1

EXHIBIT B.6a

If Yes: Did any of the following play a role in your decision to drop membership in the association you dropped most recently?

(Respondents selected up to five choices. Shown in order with most frequently selected reasons first.)

	%
Did not receive the expected value to justify the cost of dues	56.1
Change of career focus	25.6
Dissatisfied with association performance	20.7
Change of professional interest	20.2
Employer stopped paying membership dues	18.4
Association was ineffective in representing your field	17.3
Not enough local programs offered	17.3
Change of job	17.0
The group was not the right one for me	13.9
Dissatisfied with the local chapter	9.6
Disagreed with association's political/advocacy positions	9.2
Change of residence	8.6
Did not feel welcomed in the group	6.2
Change of local chapter relationship with association	2.4

Would you say that there are too many associations in your professional area of interest, too few, or is the number about right?

	%
Too Many	12.3
Too Few	9.0
About Right	63.0
Can't Say	*15.8*
	100.0

EXHIBIT B.8

Do you think there will be a greater or lesser need for associations five years from now?

	%
Greater	34.5
Lesser	8.3
About the Same	46.2
Can't Say	*11.0*
	100.0

Part Two:
About the Context of a Specific Organization

The following questions were asked in the context of a specific organization. Results are shown with all named organizations aggregated.

EXHIBIT B.9

How IMPORTANT* were [would be] the following personal benefits in your decision to join [name co-sponsor]? AND How SATISFIED† are you with [name] in delivering that benefit/service to you?
(Rated on 1-5 scale with 5=very important/very satisfied. Shown in order with most important first.)

	Mean Importance Rating	Mean Satisfaction Rating	Gap Analysis: Satisfaction Minus Importance
Access to the most up to date information available in your field	4.22	4.11	-0.10
Professional development or educational program offerings	3.91	3.95	0.03
Opportunities for you to network with other professionals in your field	3.72	3.89	0.15
Access to career information and employment opportunities	3.39	3.73	0.37
Access to products, services, and suppliers (e.g. insurance, publications, etc.)	3.21	3.75	0.63
Opportunities to gain leadership experience	3.05	3.57	0.52
A reference directory of members/ practitioners	2.93	3.73	0.85
Member discounts or group purchasing activities	2.85	3.45	0.83
Mean Importance Index‡	3.40		

* Both members and nonmembers were asked importance parts of this question.

† Only members were asked the satisfaction parts of this question and GAP analysis based only on MEMBER responses.

‡ The mean importance index is the average importance rating for all variables in this group. While adding all averages reported above and dividing by the number of variables will result in a figure close to the rating shown, the mean importance index is more accurate because the average is calculated for each respondent individually and then indexed.

How IMPORTANT* were [would be] the following benefits to your field or profession in your decision to join *[name co-sponsor]*? AND How SATISFIED† are you with *[name]* in delivering that benefit/service to your field or profession?

(Rated on 1-5 scale with 5=very important/very satisfied. Shown in order with most important first.)

	Mean Importance Rating	Mean Satisfaction Rating	Gap Analysis: Satisfaction Minus Importance
Providing standards or guidelines that support quality	3.85	3.95	0.13
Gathering, analyzing, and publishing data on trends in the field	3.77	3.97	0.25
Maintaining a code of ethics for practice	3.74	4.01	0.30
Promoting a greater appreciation of the role and value of the field among practitioners	3.70	3.79	0.10
Conducting research on significant issues affecting the field	3.70	3.87	0.24
Promoting greater public awareness of contributions in the field	3.67	3.59	-0.03
Influencing legislation and regulations that affect the field	3.64	3.73	0.15
Supporting student education and entry into the field	3.58	3.82	0.28
Attracting competent people into the field	3.53	3.65	0.20
Certifying those who meet critical competency standards	3.52	3.85	0.38
The association's role in defining critical competencies	3.44	3.80	0.40
Providing awards or recognition for excellence in the field	3.07	3.82	0.81
Mean Importance Index‡	3.63		

*Both members and nonmembers were asked importance parts of this question.

† Only members were asked the satisfaction parts of this question and GAP analysis based only on MEMBER responses.

‡ The mean importance index is the average importance rating for all variables in this group. While adding all averages reported above and dividing by the number of variables will result in a figure close to the rating shown, the mean importance index is more accurate because the average is calculated for each respondent individually and then indexed.

How did you first learn about *[name co-sponsor]*?

(Respondents selected one choice. Shown with most frequently selected first.)

	%
Colleague or co-worker	34.1
Professor or instructor	26.2
University or college program	12.1
A workshop, conference or meeting	6.1
Advertisement in a journal or magazine	3.9
Browsing on the Internet	2.6
Direct contact from the association by postal mail	2.5
Direct contact from the association electronically	0.8
Direct contact from the association in person	0.6
Booth at a trade show	0.4
Telephone or email inquiry	0.3
News story	0.1
Direct contact from the association by telephone	0.1
Do not recall	6.4
Some other way	3.8
Total	100.0

In the last 12 months, have you volunteered for *[name co-sponsor]* **in any of the following ways?**

(Check all that apply. Multiple responses permitted. Asked only of current members.)

These activities were classified into three separate variables for additional analysis. Each category is noted in the column to the right. It is important to note that respondents were permitted to select all that apply and when reclassifying into the new variable the highest level volunteer activity was predominant.

	%	
Spoke or presented a paper at a convention, regional meeting, or other educational event	10.8	Ad hoc
Served on a committee for a local chapter or section	9.4	Committee
Reviewed a paper for publication	8.5	Ad hoc
Submitted a paper for publication	7.7	Ad hoc
Served on the Board for a local chapter or section	6.0	Governance
Served on a committee for the parent organization	5.6	Committee
Served on a technical committee or special interest group	3.9	Committee
Participated in expert panel or report	2.3	Ad hoc
Prepared background for regulators, the press or others	1.2	Ad hoc
Served on the Board for the parent organization	0.8	Governance
Other	9.1	Ad hoc

	%
None of the above	69.9
Governance	6.8
Committee	7.8
Ad hoc	15.5

How likely is it that you would recommend membership in *[name co-sponsor]* **to a friend or colleague?**

(Asked only of current members.)

	%
Promoter (Rating of 9 or 10)	43.0
Passive (Rating of 7 or 8)	31.3
Detractor (Rating of 0 thru 6)	25.8
	100.0
Net Promoter Score (NPS). The result of promoter minus detractor. See *The Ultimate Question* by Fred Reichheld	17.2

Who pays your *[name co-sponsor]* **membership fee?**

(Asked only of current members.)

	%
Self	49.8
Employer	44.5
You pay part and employer pays part	2.5
Someone else	2.8
Not applicable, I am the employer	0.4
	100.0

Do you expect to renew your membership in *[name co-sponsor]* **during the next renewal cycle?**

(Asked only of current members.)

	%
Yes	92.6
No	1.1
Not Sure	6.2
	100.0

If you belong to any other associations now, would you consider *[name co-sponsor]* **your primary professional affiliation or does another association fill that role for you?**

(Asked only of current members.)

	%
Co-sponsor is primary	28.1
Other named organization is primary	17.6
None are primary	12.1
Others named/no answer	0.4
No other affiliations named	41.7
	100.0

To Nonmembers of a Specific Organization

The following questions were asked in the context of a specific organization, but only to those that were not members of the named organization. Results are shown with all named organizations aggregated.

EXHIBIT B.17

Have you ever been invited to join (or rejoin) *[name co-sponsor]***?**

	%
Yes	61.1
No	38.9
	100.0

EXHIBIT B.17a

If Yes: Which of the following invited you to join or rejoin *[name co-sponsor]***?**

(Multiple responses permitted.)

	%
A member	30.5
Someone on the association staff	44.7
Someone in the volunteer leadership of the association (not a staff member)	5.7
Someone else	23.5

EXHIBIT B.17b

If Yes: How were you contacted when you were invited to join or rejoin *[name co-sponsor]***?**

(Multiple responses permitted.)

	%
Someone contacted you in person (face to face)	20.0
By telephone	6.0
By mail	49.0
By email	37.0
In another way	7.9

How familiar are you with *[name co-sponsor]* **right now?**

	%
Very Familiar	17.3
Familiar	62.6
Have heard of it but not familiar	19.5
Never heard of it	0.6
	100.0

In the next two years do you think you will join (or rejoin) *[name co-sponsor]*?

	%
Yes	25.9
No	24.5
Don't know	49.7
	100.0

If your employer or someone else was willing to pay your membership dues for *[name co-sponsor]*, **would you join today?**

	%
Yes	64.9
No	7.1
Not sure	22.4
Not applicable (respondent is employer)	5.6

Does your employer pay for dues on your behalf to any association?

	%
Yes	28.5
No	58.0
Don't know	13.5
	100.0

Closing Questions: Demographics

The following demographic questions were asked of all respondents.

Which of the following best describes the type of organization in which you are employed?

	%
Private sector	39.2
Academia/educational institution/school	25.7
Nonprofit organization	13.5
Government	10.5
Self-employed or solo practice	9.0
Currently unemployed/between jobs	1.1
Retired	1.0
	100.0

EXHIBIT B.23

Which best describes your current career situation?
(Excludes academia, unemployed, self employed and retired)

	%
Entry level	6.0
Mid level	47.4
Senior level but not chief executive	39.9
Chief Executive	5.6

EXHIBIT B.24

What year were you born?
(Classified to age/generation label)

	%
Pre War (60 or over)	8.3
Boomers (43–59)	55.4
Gen X (30–42)	30.3
Millennials (under 30)	6.0
	100.0
Mean year	**1960**

EXHIBIT B.25

What is your gender?

	%
Male	54.8
Female	45.2
	100.0

EXHIBIT B.26

Are you a citizen of the United States?

	%
Yes	77.0
No	18.3
Not asked	4.7
	100.0

Practical Matters:
A Concise Guide to Discussion and Next Steps

THE UNDERLYING MESSAGE OF strategic imperative in *The Decision to Join* cannot be overstated. As a practical matter, absorption and application of the insight from this research happens over time and both from the helicopter level (beginning with comprehension of the findings and collection of specific data about one's own constituent pool) and on the ground (beginning with discussion and practical steps that need not wait for anything). What follows is a chapter-by-chapter (beginning with Chapter 4) compendium of implications and questions suggested for discussion in your organization.

Chapter 4: Affiliation and Involvement

Your Brand

The Decision to Join data provide valuable information that will help associations understand why some people join and others do not. But more importantly, the data show that members choose first to *affiliate* with your organization and then to engage with you. Therefore, your brand is extremely important in recruiting and keeping members. Philip Kotler, leading author and marketing expert, writes: "A brand is defined as a promise of value. It becomes the organizing concept for all the organization's activities that surround the brand."

The Decision to Join data show that members are not making their decision to join based only on a long list of personal benefits. They are joining to engage with a community of people who share a common vision. Do your membership, marketing, and communication efforts support this need to associate? The following is a list of questions you may want to consider:

- What is our brand?
- What does our association stand for?
- Whom do we represent? How are we different from everyone else in our space?
- What do we do and how do we do it?
- How do I as a member play a role in the mission of the organization?
- Can you, your staff, or your members answer these questions in 10 words or fewer? Do you have a simple, clear message that makes it easy for your members to talk about you with current and future members?
- What image comes to mind when your association name comes up? Are you the leader, the innovator, or the stable force in the industry?
- What are your core qualities and what does your organization value?
- Do your letters, brochures, Web site, and staff consistently communicate this message?
- Do you communicate to your members that they are part of a larger community and that by giving and engaging with you, they will benefit in return?
- Is the list of benefits and services targeted by segment of your membership, or does everyone get the same thing? The data show that members affiliate for a common reason but engage with you based on their personal needs. The data also show that younger members value benefits for the common good, but older members value more personal benefits.

Value and Experience

The Decision to Join shows that all three segments of the research support the overall value of associations in a very positive way. It also shows that current members and "never" members are closer in their satisfaction level than former members with current members. Former members are harder to recruit because they are basing their decision on their *experience* with your or another association while "never" members are basing their decision on the *expectation* of value. You may want to consider these questions when developing your recruitment strategy:

- How many potential members are there in your universe?
- What is your market share of this universe?
- How many are former members?
- How many are never before members?
- How many are entering the field and at what career level?
- What is the ROI on each segment for recruitment?
- How are you communicating with these segments?
- What is the potential lifetime value?

Involvement and Engagement

The data in *The Decision to Join* support what many of us know: An involved member is more likely to renew, contribute, and recruit other members than one who is not engaged with your association. The decision to promote your association to future members is the best measurement of satisfaction with your association. Identifying which members are promoters is key to growing your membership. How do you find your promoters and make it easy for them to talk about you? Consider the following:

- Do you have lists of current and former volunteers?
- Do you track their involvement similar to the ways it is done in *The Decision to Join*?
- Have you asked your current volunteers why they participate and what value they receive?

- Do you have a system for getting members involved with you?
- Is it transparent to members how they can participate and join your leadership?
- Do you offer tools and resources that make it easy for your members to talk about you?
- Do you encourage or reward them for promoting your organization?
- Do you use other volunteers to actively solicit new volunteers?
- Do you communicate the value of participation?
- Do you have data on how your members want to engage with you?
- Do you offer different levels of engagement similar to that referenced in *The Decision to Join*?

Go to www.womma.org to learn more about how to get your members to talk about you.

Chapter 5: Generations and Career Level

Associations should be very excited about the next generation of recruits waiting in the ranks. Both *The Decision to Join* and *Generations and the Future of Association Participation,* published by The William E. Smith Institute for Association Research in 2006, present a positive picture—albeit with some caveats—for the recruitment and retention of young people within your organizations. Before comparing the research to your organization, a careful analysis of your future members and current members by age and career level will provide the answers you need to engage them. The data clearly demonstrate that the perception of value changes with age and career experience. Following is a series of questions to consider as you determine how your association can put *The Decision to Join* survey data to work in making a stronger appeal to younger generational age groups and/or those in early career stages.

- Have you done a market analysis?
- Is your profession on the up-and-coming list of professions or are you a "dying breed," losing young people to another field or industry? Have you compared the number of young people entering the field to previous years, and what are the environmental trends affecting this migration?

- Or is your association the "hot new area" and you are seeing increasing numbers of young people participating in student chapters and local chapters? What is causing this increased interest in your profession?
- How many are actually entering the profession and where are they coming from?
- How are they learning about your association? What are all the access points, and are you controlling the message?
- What is your message and how is your brand conveying the promise of value to them?
- Does your message communicate the mission and value of your association to the society? How are you promoting your association to the general public? Are you creating public awareness about the profession? The data show that younger members are concerned about these questions, and it may stem from their need to have their career choice validated by the association. As they grow in their careers, association value shifts from the "good of the order" to "what's in it for me."
- What is the ROI to your association of recruiting younger members? Is it worth the increased costs to recruit them, even if they are not heavy purchasers of your products? The data show that as members grow in their career, so does their engagement with their association. This is a strong business case for considering the lifetime value of a younger member and not just their spending with you today.
- If not financial, what role do younger members play or can they play within your association? Are you prepared to engage them in leadership roles and give them a voice?
- What resources and benefits are targeted toward younger members who are early in their careers? *The Decision to Join* shows that one of the major performance gaps for the youngest age group (under 30) centered on professional development and educational program offerings.
- What opportunities do you offer to connect younger members with their peers or other early careerists? The research shows that opportunities to connect and network with other practitioners within the

field consistently ranked highest in importance to early careerists compared to other age groups.

- Since younger members do not have the financial means to travel and attend in-person meetings, how will you respond to their need to connect? Associations can use the data findings to make a case for leveraging new educational and social networking technologies to create accessible, focused networking opportunities.

Chapter 6: Gender

The existence of a dominant gender within an association has a direct impact on the reception by members and prospects of its messages and actions. This could affect your organization's ability to recruit new members, retain existing members, and engage all members in essential volunteer and leadership activities.

Before you can apply any of the findings from *The Decision to Join* to your association you must answer the following questions:

- Is your organization male-dominant, female-dominant, or integrated?
- Will there be any significant changes in this trend over the next ten years?
- Does your organization effectively communicate the areas of high value as identified by the various segments including gender?

Once you've identified the gender distribution of your organization, you are ready to consider the impact of the gender-related findings from this study.

If membership is the lifeblood of your organization, then serious consideration should be given to preferences of your membership based on various segments, such as gender. The recruitment and retention of new members can be classified in two ways: organization-driven (direct mail, Web site, email, etc) and member-driven (word of mouth). Understanding what your audience values and communicating that through your recruitment efforts should increase the success rates from your efforts. The data from the research indicates subtle yet important differences regarding the challenges faced by professions when segmented by gender. Using the data gleaned from this study and one specifically applied to your members, consider the following:

- Is there a gap between importance and satisfaction regarding environmental challenges based on gender? Could this gap be closed with better communication about your organization's efforts and offerings?
- Does your organization adequately promote the role and value of the profession to your members? How satisfied are your members with your performance on this issue?
- How important is gathering, analyzing, and publishing data on trends in the field to your organization and its members? How satisfied are your members with your performance on this issue?
- How important is it to your members that your organization conduct research on significant issues affecting the field? How satisfied are your members with your performance on this front?
- Do you offer a certification within the profession? Is this valued by your members?
- How are issues related to advocacy prioritized within your organization? Are your members aware of your advocacy efforts?
- Do your recruitment messages emphasize the environmental challenges that are important to your membership base (based on gender)?
- Are your members in a position to "tell a friend" about membership—and are they given the tools to facilitate this action? Can you tailor your messages to emphasize the personal benefits that rank high in value to your audience based on various segments?
- Do you know what percentage of each gender holds various volunteer positions within your organization when cross-tabulated by age group and career stage (CEO, senior staff, mid-level, and entry-level)?
- Are the roles and responsibilities of the various volunteer jobs aligned with the interests of your members?

Chapter 7: Employer Type and Level of Support

Employer Type

Think through these questions:

- Who are your members? What is the membership breakdown by employer type relative to The Decision to Join study?

- Of the employer types, nonprofits are the least satisfied with associations' ability to meet their expectations in delivering professional development and education and in providing standards or guidelines that support quality. How do your nonprofit members rate your association's performance in these areas? Have you reviewed and compared the data from your session evaluations by employer type? Do you know what percentage of nonprofit members uses your association's educational and professional development programs?

- Academic members are more likely to belong to associations and less likely to drop association memberships when compared to other employer types. They are less apt to change careers, more willing to volunteer, and most likely to be an association's biggest promoter. How can your association best tap into this membership segment even if they are a minority segment of your membership? Consider targeting academic members as promoters/recruiters for your association. This can be done at meetings, specialized campaigns, and so forth. Academic members prefer to receive information from the association at conferences or meetings. Consider asking academic members to invite prospective academic members to your meetings and creating programs on site specific to this membership segment considering the association functions they rate highest in importance in The Decision to Join study: representing the field to the public, representing the field to the government, connecting practitioners within the field to each other, and providing timely information about the field.

Level of Support

The impact of who pays the membership dues on the decision to join is an ongoing debate in membership circles. For those organizations that have a golden handcuff—that is, the member has to be a member to practice his or her profession—it does not matter. But for associations in which members pay their own dues, the cost versus value equation is always a factor. In other organizations, where either the employer or employee may pays the dues, another set of circumstances arise. The data suggest that the association may need to develop a relationship with both parties to keep the membership growing.

The Decision to Join considers all three scenarios and gives you an understanding of how who pays the dues may affect your recruitment and retention strategies. Before you can apply these findings to your association, you must answer the following questions:

- Do you know who pays for the membership dues for your members or what percentage of your members' dues are paid by the employer versus the individual member? Can you query your membership if you don't know or are unsure? This can be done through applications and renewals, polls, meetings, and so forth.

- When individual members pay for their own dues, they tend to have a less favorable attitude toward associations, expect more ROI from their association memberships, are more likely to believe associations perform poorly in addressing some of the challenges they face, and are more likely to drop their association memberships. The data also indicate that those who don't join would if their employer paid the dues. How can your association strategically address ways to build value and increase membership considering the factor of who pays for the dues? How does your association create its appeals to individual dues-paying members to increase the ROI and value? How can you use the survey data compared to the dues structure of your association membership to identify and take advantage of opportunities and improve on weaknesses?

- If your membership is split on dues payment, what percentage of your members pay their own dues, and what percentage is paid by the employer?

- Does this have an impact on your renewal rates? Who renews at a higher rate?

- How does the dues payment affect a member's engagement with you?

- If the employer pays the dues, do the members attend more programs and purchase more products?

- Do members who pay their own dues use your Web site, knowledge resources, and similar benefits more than other members?
- Does the dues question affect their involvement with your association? If yes, how do they differ in their involvement with you?

All these questions are important to understanding how your members make decisions and how they determine their value. *The Decision to Join* addresses the myth that members who pay their own way really appreciate their membership more than others. What the data really show is that they can be your most loyal members and your most loyal critics. As for employers who pay member dues, the message is clear that you must understand your member's business like your own to make a concise argument for membership in your association.

Chapter 8: World Location

Under pressure to increase membership, many associations have looked at the international market as a way to build their numbers. This is often done without careful market analysis and assessment of the ROI of bringing in these new members. *The Decision to Join* provides the data to help you understand these future international members. Here are some questions that you may want to consider:

- How many international members do you have now?
- What is the potential universe of international members?
- Do you break them down by country and continent?
- Do you have the data on how they engage with you?
- Do they attend learning programs?
- Do they purchase books?
- What are the customer service challenges in servicing them? Do these challenges include language, shipping, standards, dollar exchange, etc.?
- Do you offer them both electronic and print communications?
- Have you considered an e-membership?
- Have you done a cost-benefit analysis of your benefits and services?
- What type of learning programs can you offer international members?

- Since networking is the top reason for joining, how do you facilitate engagement for the international community? Who pays for it?
- How do you welcome international members to your association meetings?
- Do you have ways for them to engage with you since this is the number one reason for joining?
- Do you have a technology platform that allows for communication among members?

Next Steps

Once you've discussed and answered the questions in this appendix and created a clear picture of your membership (and potential universe), consider the impact any changes will have on the strategic direction of the organization. If you've uncovered barriers to entry, consider the impact on the changing demographics of your organization should you remove those barriers. Once you've expanded your membership base, it is inevitable that the areas of high interest may change. Is your organization willing and able to make those changes? The sweet spot for an organization is the intersection of relevance, market opportunities, and organizational capacities. Making changes based on your own organization's research findings may change that equation.

For example, if your organization is predominantly senior career-stage individuals and you wish to expand to early career-stage, you will be changing the value proposition because the conversation at the meetings and in the publications must address all audiences. This could be true for any type of segment. This clearly demonstrates why being data centric, measure 3 in the ASAE & The Center research study and publication *7 Measures of Success: What Remarkable Associations Do That Others Don't* (2006), gives you the information to analyze your situation and make strategic decisions that will grow your association.

This appendix was provided by the 2006-2007 Membership Section Council. The "Next Steps" section was contributed by Sheri Jacobs, CAE, 2006-2007 Chairman, ASAE & The Center Membership Section Council. Special recognition goes to Sheri, of McKinley Marketing, and the following individuals for their roles in preparing this appendix:

Stuart Meyer, CAE   *Emergency Nurses Association*
Shelley Sanner, CAE   *American Council on Education*
Sharon Moss   *American Speech-Language-Hearing Association*
Carylann Pishner   *ASAE & The Center*

A Guide to Conducting the Study in an Individual Membership Organization

Introduction

THE DECISION TO JOIN examines the powerful psychogenic need for affiliation in the context of association membership. This ground-breaking study addresses the most critical question in individual membership organizations: Why do some individuals join and affiliate with associations while others do not?

This guide and the survey template files available for purchase online at **www.asaecenter.org/decisiontojoin** are intended to help organizations that wish to administer The Decision to Join survey to their own members and nonmembers. This guide describes the methodology used and provides directions on data analysis and instructions for benchmarking against the results presented in the book. The survey materials available online include questionnaire templates, customizable cover letters for both member and nonmembers, and the pooled data against which organizations that undertake the study may compare against the data they receive. The purpose is to provide all the information that an association would need to conduct a Decision to Join study on its own.

The pooled benchmarking data were compiled with the help of 18 diverse individual membership organizations that were among the study's initial co-sponsors. This diversity of organizations ensured that a wide variety of individuals was included so that the results about how individuals make decisions to join individual membership organizations can be applied to the general population. The initial benchmarking data include responses from 16,944 individuals. We will update the benchmarking data as new results are added to the database.

In addition to the relationship respondents have with the 18 co-sponsoring organizations, a majority of them reported current memberships in other membership organizations and specifically named more than 13,000 memberships in 5,000 different associations in every possible description and size category. Members of local, state, and regional associations, and professional, fraternal, user, and business groups in associations of all sizes are included in this sample.

In providing this step-by-step guide to conducting The Decision to Join for your organization, we are hoping to significantly increase the size of this database. Contributing your data to this large database will help to advance knowledge about why individuals join membership organizations. Knowing more about what motivates people to join or not join individual membership organizations will help all membership organizations to target the most compelling membership appeal and spot trends across time. If you wish to contribute results, we have provided the required file structure (see MS Excel files titled "Member and Nonmember Database Field Names1") in the survey template files available online.

ASAE & The Center
Decision to Join Consulting Services

In the spirit of advancing knowledge in association management, this guide and the survey templates can be used by any organization wishing to administer the survey in-house or using an outside consultant. We also offer a full-service option, similar to the program we offered to the original 18 co-sponsors. This option includes the following:

- A statistically valid survey of your organization's members and nonmembers
- Complete Internet implementation
- Questions identical to those in the original questionnaires and an opportunity for you to include two custom questions
- Custom statistical report benchmarking results for your organization against all other individual membership organizations in the database up to that point
- A database of responses for your organization

For organizations conducting the study on their own, ASAE & The Center offer custom benchmarking services that will allow comparison of

your organization's data against the entire database by key demographic categories:

- Joiners and non-Joiners
- Age by generation including large samples of Baby Boomers, Gen Xers and Millennials
- Residency in or outside the United States and/or North America
- Gender, including women and men in gender-dominated organizations (organizations in which one gender makes up 75 percent or more of members)
- Employment sector, including private sector, government, academia, and nonprofit organizations (We also have a large sub-sample of sole practitioners in the private sector.)
- Career situation, including CEOs, senior managers, and entry level
- Those whose employers pay dues and those who pay dues from their own pocket
- Volunteer and non-volunteer members
- Members who can be considered "promoters" of their organizations

Please contact the Industry & Market Research Department at ASAE & The Center for Association Leadership if you wish to learn more about turnkey administration or custom benchmarking for The Decision to Join. Your purchase price for the book The Decision to Join and the survey templates will be recognized as a discount on fees charged for turnkey administration or custom benchmarking. Additionally, please contact the Industry & Market Research Department if you need assistance using the information in this guide or the survey templates to conduct your own Decision to Join study.

Conducting The Decision to Join Study
For Your Organization

The major tasks in any survey project are shown in the following model. This workbook is organized by these tasks. Readers requiring general information about survey research methods should consult The Survey Research

Handbook, 3rd Edition, by Pamela L. Alreck and Robert B. Settle, Irwin, 2004.

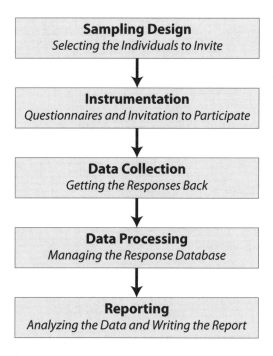

Sampling Design
Selecting the Individuals to Invite

The Decision to Join study is designed for individual membership organizations that must compete for members. Organizations in which membership is required to practice in the profession represented or those in which members represent a vast majority of the market are not good candidates for this study.

The study is intended to be administered to members and nonmembers concurrently. Organizations with small memberships (less than 1,000) should plan to use a census approach (all members are invited to participate) while those with larger memberships should use a random representative sampling approach.

The goal of most organizations should be to receive a total of between 350 and 400 completed questionnaires. Having 350-400 completed responses is standard in the primary market research field and provides associations with approximately a 95 percent confidence level with a margin-of-error of plus or minus 5 percent. You may determine your association's exact margin of error by using any number of free Internet margin-of-error calculators; a link to one is
www.sciencebuddies.org/mentoring/project_ideas/Soc_participants.shtml

A total of 350-400 responses to each of the two versions of the questionnaire (member and nonmember) is ideal if the only comparisons of interest are between the two groups. If further demographic breakdowns are desired, a larger sample of the desired demographic group is needed.

In the original study, for example, the sponsors wanted to look at two sub-groups among nonmembers: those who were former members and those who had never been members. To have confidence in the findings of each of these two sub-groups, a larger number of nonmembers was required. If these sub-groups are important in your study, please remember to increase your nonmember sample size.

Assuming sampling is appropriate, the most desirable sampling method is random representative sampling throughout the entire population. This can be achieved either by using a software program that includes "random selection" (SPSS, SAS and Microsoft Excel all have modules like this) or using "nth number sampling." "Nth number sampling is simple. For example, if you have 1,000 members and want a sample of 300 from that group, you select every third name in the list (1,000 divided by 300). A random representative sample will allow you to take your findings and generalize to your whole population.

Using either method, the appropriate sample is arrived at by multiplying the number of responses required by the expected response rate. The expected response rate should be estimated by using an average response rate received in past surveys of the applicable population. For organizations with 5,000 or fewer names to choose from (e.g., members or nonmembers, as applicable) a sample size of 350 will be sufficient. For organizations with more than 5,000 in the total population, a sample size of 400 will be sufficient. These sample sizes will result in statistical confidence at approximately 95 percent with a margin-of-error of plus or minus 5 percent.

Confidence is the probability that the sample reflects the population and margin of error is the interval around which results are accurate.

Here is an example of calculating the sample needed based on the following assumptions:

- Number of members = 4,000
- Average response rate in previous surveys of members = 25 percent
- Number of individuals needed in random select to yield 350 responses = 1,400. (If using the nth method, selecting every 3rd member will result in a sample of 1,333—the closest you will get to the required 1,400, since you cannot choose a fraction of an individual. Of course, you could also choose every second member with a resulting 2,000 in the sample and then randomly remove 600 from that group.)

Instrumentation
Questionnaires and Invitation to Participate

Both the member and nonmember questionnaires used in the original Decision to Join study are part of the survey templates available for purchase online at **www.asaecenter.org/decisiontojoin**. **If your organization intends to benchmark against the original study and/or wishes to contribute to The Decision to Join database, question wording may not be changed.** Questions may be added (custom questions), and questions or parts of multi-part questions may be deleted entirely but wording must remain exactly as shown.

For example, some of the original Decision to Join organizations omitted the demographic question on race (question 28 in the member version and 31 in the nonmember version) and others, whose membership was entirely based in the United States, omitted questions on national origin (question 27-29 in the member version and 30-32 in the nonmember version). You should include those questions that are of value to your organization while deleting those with no value.

Questions 1 through 11 in both the member and nonmember versions of the survey are the same and generic, referring to associations in general, not your organization in particular. This series of questions provides information about the individual's attitude toward the role and function of associations as a group and is important to set the stage for collecting information about attitudes toward your organization in particular.

Following question 11 in both the nonmember and member versions of the questionnaire, respondents are directed to questions referring to your organization in particular. Here you will need to insert your organization's name in questions as appropriate.

Survey instrumentation also includes the following items that should be prepared by your organization. The cover emails used in the original study are provided for guidance.

- Cover letter (or email depending on data collection method selected)
- Follow-up reminder letter or email
- Postage-paid return envelope for mail data collection (do not omit a postage-paid return envelope if postal mail is used, because your response rate will suffer)

Data Collection
Getting the Responses Back

This study was designed for either Internet or postal mail distribution. To maximize response, you may use both methods concurrently. If using Internet alone, you must have good email addresses for all potential respondents; otherwise you are introducing bias into your sampling plan, since not all individuals in the total list would have an equal chance of receiving the questionnaire. In the original study, most organizations used an email-only method of data collection.

Regardless of the method selected to collect data, at least one original invitation and one follow-up to non-respondents should be planned. *For this reason, there should be some way to identify non-respondents to the original mailing.* This means that you may not promise anonymity in your cover letter or email. You *should* promise (and adhere) to confidentiality. (Recall, there is a major difference between anonymity and confidentiality. Anonymity means there is no way to identify the individual who responded while confidentiality means that you may be able to identify the individual but you will not share identifying information with others.)

In an Internet deployment, the follow-up should be a week to 10 days after the initial deployment. If you use the ASAE-endorsed program for Internet deployment, we can provide a template for the questionnaires directly to your account, which will save considerable time for you. Contact the Industry & Market Research Department at ASAE & The Center for contact information. For mail, a two-to-three-week interval is suggested. From past experience, the second postal mailing should include another full copy of the questionnaire. A follow-up note without a questionnaire or a simple postcard has been found not to be as effective.

You may prefer to offer a respondent incentive, although anything other than an incentive included in the envelope with an original mailing has not been empirically shown to be effective. In the original study we offered a drawing for one of three American Express gift cards. This proved difficult because these are not permitted for use outside the United States. If respondents outside the United States are expected, incentive delivery issues must be anticipated. In future deployments we would recommend omitting a respondent incentive

Data Processing
Managing the Response Database

If Internet is used for data collection, responses should be downloaded and reviewed at least several times weekly to ensure that data collection and skip patterns are working properly.

If postal mail is selected as the method of data collection, a survey editor should be responsible for reviewing responses before they are provided to data entry personnel. This entails reviewing each returned questionnaire to ensure that all questions are answered appropriately. A typical issue that would be resolved in editing is when the respondent answers questions about why they dropped a membership, for example, without checking the Yes/No question on having dropped a membership. In this case, the editor would simply check the 'Yes' alternative since it can be inferred that a membership was dropped in the past if the respondent gives reasons for doing that.

Regardless of the method of data collection, it is also important to weed out inappropriate or incomplete questionnaires. This initial editorial step will facilitate accurate data entry and analysis. You can generally spot inappropriate responses by visual review. For example, when it is clear in scaled questions that the respondent simply circled one number in the scale for all answers, correction is required. This is easy to spot in visual inspection but difficult to detect after data entry. When this occurs the editor should instruct data entry to consider all these responses as "missing" or no answer.

Incompletes are more subjective. Some unanswered questions should be expected in most responses, but well more than half of the questions are required for a response to be included in the final database. You should decide on the rules for incompletes before deploying the survey and stick to those rules throughout. The use of statistical software (e.g., SPSS or SAS) is encouraged because it will make data and analysis easier, but any spreadsheet or database program (e.g., Microsoft Excel) can be used for data entry.

One of the most important aspects of data entry is setting up your data entry spreadsheet properly. Every data point should be in a separate field. For example, in a question like number 3: *"What do you think are the most important functions of an association? (Please check up to three choices.)"* Each of the 10 options should be in a separate column, not in one column with three answers or three columns with any response number within range. Similarly, "other" and the verbatim comments that might follow must also be separated. A good rule of thumb is that if the question is limited to one response (i.e., respondents were only allowed to check one answer), one column is needed to record responses. If a question has multiple responses (i.e., respondents were permitted to check more than one answer), a separate column for each possible response alternative is needed.

Care should also be taken in contingent questions like questions 7 and 8 that the column designated for answers to 8 are blank (not 0, for example) in cases where question 7 is "no" and question 8 is skipped.

Attention to data processing and establishing and keeping rules consistently will make data analysis and reporting much simpler and increase confidence in your results. **Strict adherence to the file structure provided with the survey templates is required if you wish to benchmark against the original data.**

Reporting
Analyzing the Data and Writing the Report

A number of post-data collection variables have been created in The Decision to Join analysis plan, among others, the following:

- Generation based on year born (questions 25 in member and 28 in nonmember versions)
- World location based on responses to citizenship and residency
- Governance versus other types of volunteer (question 19 in the member version)
- Member status (never members and former members) based on Question 14 in the nonmember version

Assuming your sample size is the minimum recommended in sampling, as described earlier, differences of 5 percent or greater between member and nonmember results should be considered the rule of thumb for reporting differences between the two survey populations (members and nonmembers). This is a rule of thumb. If you would like to report statistically significant differences, the aid of a statistical program will be needed.

If you are using SPSS for analysis, ASAE & The Center Industry & Market Research can provide the syntax necessary for both creating new variables and analyzing data.

At minimum, we recommend preparing cross-tabulation tables in the format shown in tables that are provided in the survey templates. This report template provides columns for reporting data in the detail that we provided to the initial study participants. This template is provided in Microsoft Excel format. Three worksheets provide all benchmark data for all respondents, members, and nonmembers. Nonmembers are further broken out by former members and never members. Using cross-tabulations is a relatively easy way to show the results to non-statisticians and a good place to start the reporting and the discussion with key staff and volunteer leaders.

Additional analysis on generation and career stage, world location, level of activity, and employer type as appropriate would be the next level of reporting and insight.

Decision to Join Benchmarking Opportunities

As an incentive for organizations to provide their results to ASAE & The Center's database, we will provide ad hoc telephone consultation free of charge throughout 2008 if you wish to undertake the study in-house or use your own consultant. This will include specific guidance on all of the tasks necessary to complete this study. If SPSS is used for analysis, we will also provide our file structure parameters and the syntax files necessary to create new variables and generate cross-tab tables. After 2008, please call ASAE & The Center Industry & Market Research Department to confirm that this offer remains in effect.

This complementary consultation service will only be available for organizations that provide information in the appropriate format (the file structure requirements included in the survey templates available for purchase online) in Microsoft Excel or ASCII format and agree to allow their data to be added to our Decision to Join database.

Additional analysis can also be provided on a fee-for-service basis. Fee-for-service options are as follows:

- Basic analysis on your data, returning your tables in an Excel file benchmarked against the original database
- Creation of new variables for generation, world location, member status (more finely tuned than member nonmember), gender-dominant profession or field, and volunteer level
- Statistical tests of significance by any of the key demographics
- Written narrative reports of findings

We also offer a turnkey service for The Decision to Join in which we will conduct the survey on behalf of your organization. If you take this service, we will deduct the price you paid for the book and survey templates from your fee. This full-service option is available through 2008 for $15,000. After 2008, please contact ASAE & The Center Industry & Market Research Department to confirm that this offer remains in effect at this price. The following services are included:

- Two statistically valid surveys of your organization's members and nonmembers

- Identical questions to those used with the initial co-sponsoring organizations, and an opportunity to include two custom questions

- Internet deployment up to 8,500 individuals for whom email addresses are available. If implementation by postal mail is preferred we will handle the mailings but direct charges associated with printing, postage and data entry will be charged at cost. Both Internet and mail deployments will include one original and one follow-up posting to non-respondents.

- Custom statistical report benchmarking results for your organization against other organizations in the study

- A database of responses for your organization in Excel, ASCII and/or SPSS 15.0 format

The following materials are provided in the survey template downloads available at **www.asaecenter.org/decisiontojoin**:

- The Decision to Join Questionnaires: templates for the member and nonmember version of The Decision to Join study. These templates are also available through the ASAE-endorsed electronic survey vendor. If you do the survey in house or with your own consultant or vendor, these templates can be downloaded to an account that you set up with that vendor separately. Contact ASAE & The Center Industry & Market Research Department if you wish to use this option.

- Samples of the cover letters or emails used for the invitation to participate in the survey

- Microsoft Excel column format requirements

- Microsoft Excel report template which contains the pooled data showing results for all organizations that have completed the study to date. This file is set up so that your organization can use it to insert its own data in the columns provided.

For more information, contact the ASAE & The Center Industry & Market Research Department at 202-626-2744 or evaluations@asaecenter.org. If email, please refer to "Decision to Join" in your subject line.

Index

About the Authors

James Dalton, president of Strategic Counsel, is a management consultant to the nonprofit community with specialties in customer research, process improvement, strategic planning, and leadership development. Prior to establishing his consulting practice, Dalton served as chief executive officer of the American Society of Landscape Architects, where he instituted an ongoing member research program to gather information on member satisfaction, changing market dynamics, and emerging issues that define the needs of the profession. He also spent 18 years at the National Society of Professional Engineers, where he served in a number of roles including that of deputy executive director. Dalton has been an active volunteer in ASAE & The Center for Association Leadership and has acted as a primary author and contributor on the topic of strategic planning and leadership. His works include *From Scan to Plan: Managing Change in Associations* and *From Scan to Plan: Integrating Trends into the Strategy-Making Process.* He was a member of ASAE & The Center's Measures of Success Task Force, whose multi-year efforts resulted in the landmark *7 Measures of Success: What Remarkable Associations Do That Others Don't,* published in 2006. Previously, as a member of the ASAE Foundation Research Committee, he served as liaison to the Wharton School on a collaborative project investigating the strategy-making process in associations.

Monica Dignam is vice president, Industry and Market Research at ASAE & The Center for Association Leadership. She has been a professional researcher for more than 30 years. Before coming to ASAE & The Center in 2004, Dignam was president of Monalco, Inc., a Milwaukee firm specializing in research for associations. She was also an active volunteer, serving on the ASAE Marketing Section Council and contributing both as a writer and as a speaker to ASAE & The Center and a number of allied societies of association executives. Dignam is a past board member of Professional Dimensions, a Milwaukee professional women's group, and a founding member of the Washington area's Women in Advertising and Marketing. She is also a member of the Qualitative Research Consultants Association and the Association for Research on Nonprofit Organizations and Voluntary Action.

About ASAE & The Center for Association Leadership

If you're already a member, you know that publications are but a small part of what ASAE & The Center for Association Leadership offer. If you aren't a member, we'd like you to know that ASAE & The Center are a rich community of people united by a shared commitment to association leadership and management. We connect great ideas and great people to inspire leadership and achievement in the association community. Our promise is to provide exceptional experiences, a vibrant community, and essential tools to make you and your organization more successful. ASAE & The Center for Association Leadership are two organizations linked together by a common belief and a common passion. We believe associations have the power to transform society for the better. Our passion is to help association professionals achieve previously unimaginable levels of performance. We do this by nurturing a community of really smart, creative, and interesting people: our members.

Specifically, ASAE & The Center produce more than 75 learning experiences each year; publish *Associations Now* magazine and the *Journal of Association Leadership*; provide thousands of Web-based tools and resources; help members connect in 13 professional interest areas; conduct future-focused and market research; host ASAE & The Center's Annual Meeting & Exposition, the Great Ideas Conference, and the Springtime exposition; and act as the voice for and advocate of the association profession.

We invite you to learn more and become a part of this vibrant community.

Are you looking for innovative and improved ways to do your job?

Turn to ASAE & The Center for Association Leadership for the most comprehensive library of association industry resources; the most complete calendar of cutting-edge professional development programs; and networking opportunities with the largest gathering of association professionals and industry partners in the country.

ASAE & The Center work together to bring the most comprehensive collection of services and resources to association professionals and industry partners. ASAE enhances the many benefits of membership through publications, professional communities, and volunteer leadership opportunities. It also protects the interests of nonprofit organizations through its national advocacy and grassroots efforts. The Center for Association Leadership provides future-focused research, essential education, knowledge resources, and community that challenge and empower association professionals.

Other Titles From ASAE & The Center for Association Leadership

Visit our online bookstore at www.asaecenter.org/bookstore for these and other titles published by ASAE & The Center for Association Leadership:

7 Measures of Success: What Remarkable Associations Do That Others Don't
Association Compensation & Benefits Study
Blue Chip Compensation & Benefits Study
Association Law Handbook, 4th Edition, A Practical Guide for Associations, Societies, and Charities
Association Tax Compliance Guide
Building a Knowledge-Based Culture
Business of Certification, The
Certification and Accreditation Law Handbook, 2nd Edition
Community Building Card Deck
Core Competencies in Association Professional Development
Enhancing Committee Effectiveness: Guidelines &Policies for Committee Administration
Financial Management Handbook for Associations and Nonprofits
From Scan to Plan: Integrating Trends into the Strategy-Making Process
Fundamentals of Accreditation, The
High-Impact Governing in a Nutshell
How to Read Nonprofit Financial Statements
Letter Idea Book, The
Mapping the Future of Your Association
Membership Marketing
Membership Operations
Membership Services
Operating Ratio Report
Policies and Procedures in Association Management
Principles of Association Management, 4th ed.
Professional Practices in Association Management, 2nd Edition, An Essential Resource for Effective Management of Nonprofit Organizations
Small Staff Association Fundamentals
Strategic Planning for Association Executives
Volunteer Leadership Issue, The
Will to Govern Well, The

A Note About the Printer and the Materials Used to Produce This Book

The printer of this book recently received the Chain of Custody Certification through Bureau Veritas for both the Forest Stewardship Council (FSC) and the Sustainable Forestry Initiative (SFI). These certifications enable the printer to be a strong link in the paper supply chain starting with forestry management through the conversion of certified materials. They certify that the printer has implemented a wood products control system according to the Forest Stewardship Council certification system and they were audited and found to be in accordance with the requirements of the Sustainable Forestry Initiative® Program requirements for fiber sourcing, chain of custody, and product labels. Certification allows the printer's customers who choose FSC- or SFI-certified papers for their printed products to identify themselves as being FSC- or SFI-compliant.

With this commitment, the printer will continue to do its part to comply with Earth-friendly programs that will benefit its customers, employees, and future generations.